BEFORE THE WORLD WAS READY

STORIES OF DARING GENIUS IN SCIENCE

CLAIRE EAMER

ART BY
SA BOOTHROYD

annick press
toronto + new york + vancouver

To the scientists—many of them trailbreakers—who have generously shared their time, knowledge, and enthusiasm with me over the years—C.E.

To my sister, Gillian, who has always supported my art career, fed my kids, run my dog, and picked me up at the ferry—S.B.

Edited by Paula Ayer
Designed by Natalie Olsen, Kisscut Design
Proofread by Tanya Trafford

Annick Press Ltd.

We acknowledge the support of the Canada Council for the Arts, the Ontario Arts Council, and the Government of Canada through the Canada Book Fund (CBF) for our publishing activities.

ONTARIO ARTS COUNCIL
CONSEIL DES ARTS DE L'ONTARIO
50 YEARS OF ONTARIO GOVERNMENT SUPPORT OF THE ARTS
50 ANS DE SOUTIEN DU GOUVERNEMENT DE L'ONTARIO AUX ARTS

Cataloging in Publication

Eamer, Claire, 1947–
Before the world was ready : stories of daring genius in science /
Claire Eamer ; art by Sa Boothroyd.

Includes bibliographical references and index.
Also issued in electronic format.
ISBN 978-1-55451-536-3 (bound).—ISBN 978-1-55451-535-6 (pbk.)

1. Discoveries in science—Juvenile literature.   2. Scientists—Biography—Juvenile literature.   3. Inventors—Biography—Juvenile literature.   I. Boothroyd, Sa   II. Title.

Q180.55.D57E24 2013   j509.2'2   C2013-901213-3

Distributed in Canada by:
Firefly Books Ltd.
50 Staples Avenue, Unit 1
Richmond Hill ON L4B 0A7

Published in the U.S.A. by Annick Press (U.S.) Ltd.
Distributed in the U.S.A. by:
Firefly Books (U.S.) Inc.
P.O. Box 1338 Ellicott Station
Buffalo, NY 14205

Printed in China

Visit us at: www.annickpress.com
Visit Claire Eamer at: www.claireeamer.com
Visit Sa Boothroyd at: www.saboothroyd.com

CONTENTS

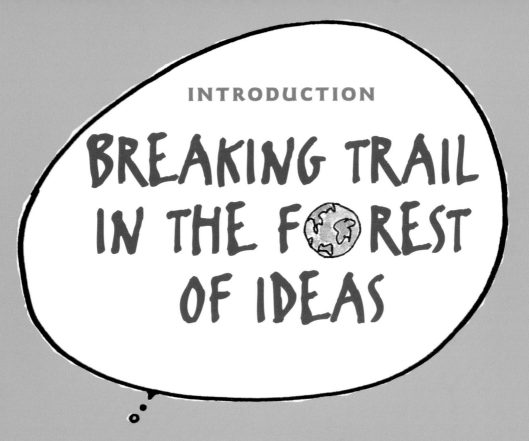

BREAKING TRAIL IN THE F🌐REST OF IDEAS

Trailbreakers have a hard job. They slog ahead, all alone. They make the trail easier for the people behind them, but they pay a price. Sometimes they even get lost along the way.

There are trailbreakers for ideas too, and they can have just as hard a time. The world isn't always ready to accept a new idea. Or new information. Or even a brilliant invention.

Sometimes, it's because the ideas make us uncomfortable. They don't match the way we see the world or ourselves. The first person to come up with an idea as outlandish as Earth revolving around the sun might not even live long enough to see it believed. In fact, that idea took almost 2,000 years to be accepted.

Some ideas are inconvenient. In the 1950s, when medical researchers said smoking causes cancer, a lot of people didn't want to believe it. Believing would mean changes. Smokers might

2

have to quit. Stores might have to sell something else. The big tobacco companies might go out of business. The tobacco companies hated the idea so much that they spent millions of dollars trying to convince people it wasn't true. Today, most people know it's true, but lots of people still smoke, either because they are addicted to tobacco or because they think they'll be lucky and not get sick.

There are other reasons why an idea might not be accepted. Sometimes a great idea comes from the wrong person. Through much of history, if a revolutionary idea came from a foreigner, a peasant, a slave, or a woman, no one paid much attention. Occasionally the person who first speaks the new idea out loud is simply bad at explaining things. The person who comes along and explains the idea clearly is more likely to be listened to— and often gets credit for the idea itself.

Sometimes a piece of the idea is missing. Alfred Wegener was sure that the continents moved around Earth's surface. He could show evidence to prove that they moved, but he couldn't explain why. Until someone came up with the *why*, people weren't ready to believe him.

And sometimes it's a simple matter of technology. It's no good inventing a rocket before a rocket motor has been developed. It's no good hunting for microbes without a microscope. Sometimes new developments, especially in technology, simply have to wait until all the bits come together.

Even then, few big ideas win wide support right away. There are always trailbreakers who had the idea before the world was prepared to believe it. And the world can be very hard on trailbreakers. In this book, you'll meet a few of them. And you'll find out what happens when the world isn't quite ready for them.

CHAPTER 1

WHAT HAVE YOU DONE TO MY PLANET?

Imagine that, all your life, you've believed Earth is the center of the universe and the sun, planets, and stars revolve around it. That's what your teachers and parents and all the people you know believe. Besides, it's obvious. You can see the proof every day, as the sun sweeps across the sky from east to west and starts again the next morning.

Then along comes someone who tells you that Earth is just a planet like all the rest, a globe that spins and whirls around the sun in the blackness of space. You'd probably think that person was wrong or crazy.

That person was Nicolaus Copernicus.

ORPHANED IN POLAND

If you search for a picture of Nicolaus Copernicus, you'll find a serious-looking man with long, dark hair that blends into the shadows behind him. He looks sidelong at the artist, a little suspiciously. That's the man who spent hours, and years, thinking about the shape of the universe.

That's not the Nicolaus Copernicus of 1483. Then, he was a grieving 10-year-old whose father, a copper merchant in northern Poland, had just died. His mother was already dead, so Nicolaus and his older brother and two older sisters were orphans. The children went to live with their uncle Lukas, a priest, and their lives changed.

Amount of time Copernicus spent thinking about the shape of the universe

Amount of time he spent thinking about his hairstyle

Uncle Lukas was so serious that even when you tickled him under his toes, he continued to frown.

Lukas Watzenrode was a serious man—so serious that it was said he never laughed. But he was a responsible uncle. He decided to prepare Nicolaus and his brother, Andreas, for respectable jobs as church officials. The boys were sent to a good school and then to university, first in Poland and later in Italy. Nicolaus studied philosophy, mathematics, astronomy, astrology, medicine, and church law. In Italy, he lectured in astronomy for a while.

MOVING IN THE WRONG CIRCLES

In school, Nicolaus Copernicus learned about a system called the Ptolemaic universe. Some 1,400 years earlier, the Greek-Egyptian astronomer Ptolemy had written that Earth was the unmoving center of the universe, and the sun, stars, and planets revolved around it. At some point in his studies, however, Copernicus began to have doubts.

The problem was the planets. They don't sweep smoothly across the sky as you might expect if they were circling Earth. Instead, they wander around the sky, sometimes even going backward for a while and then shifting direction again.

What astronomers thought was happening in the universe:

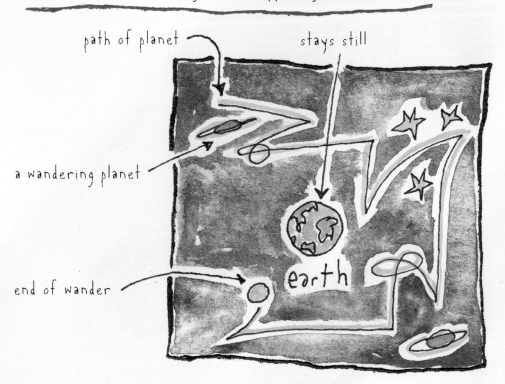

path of planet

stays still

a wandering planet

end of wander

earth

Astronomers measured their movements carefully and developed complicated theories to explain their motion. But the more they studied the planets and the more they learned, the harder it was to fit what they saw into Ptolemy's model of the universe.

In 1503, Copernicus returned to Poland, still puzzling over the wandering planets. He worked as a church official and the personal doctor of his uncle Lukas, now a powerful bishop, but that didn't keep him from astronomy. Once his workday was done, Copernicus read, calculated, and thought about the bright, mysterious lights in the night sky.

Aristarchus Measures the Sun

About 260 BCE, on the Greek island of Samos, an astronomer named Aristarchus figured out how to calculate the size of the sun. He didn't get the numbers quite right— all he had to work with was a measuring stick and a really good head for math!—but he realized that the sun is huge, far larger than Earth. In fact, it's so big that the idea of the sun revolving around Earth just didn't make sense. It would be like a monkey swinging a full-grown elephant around in the air, instead of the elephant swinging the monkey. So Aristarchus came up with a new theory. The sun, he said, is the center of the universe, and Earth revolves around it. Most people, even his fellow astronomers, thought that was nonsense, and the idea was abandoned in Europe for more than 1,800 years—until Copernicus.

COPERNICUS DOES THE MATH

At some point, his thoughts turned in a new direction. He asked himself, what if those puzzling planets don't revolve around Earth at all? What if they move around the sun? And what if Earth also revolves around the sun? That was a daring idea. Too daring. He needed evidence.

But how to get the evidence? Copernicus couldn't send a rocket into space to take a look. He couldn't even look through a telescope; it hadn't been invented yet. But he could use his imagination, and mathematics. He drew a diagram of how he pictured the solar system, with the sun at its center and the planets—Earth included—circling around it. Then he used math to calculate what the planets' movements would look like from Earth.

MY NEW SOLAR SYSTEM, by Nic

Some of Copernicus's diagrams were big and hard to hide.

Suddenly, the movements he saw in the night sky made sense. The planets' apparently aimless wandering was simply their change in position relative to a moving Earth. When a planet appeared to move backward in the sky, it meant that Earth, which was also zipping around the sun, had caught up with that planet and passed it.

The sky made even more sense if Earth was not only revolving around the sun, but also rotating on its own axis. That would explain the rise and set of the sun and the behavior of the stars, which appear to sweep across the sky each night. *They* weren't moving. *Earth* was.

The more he thought about it, the more Copernicus was sure he was right. But he also knew that he had come up with a dangerous idea. In those days, the Christian church was a major force in European life and politics, and, like many religions, Christianity taught that Earth and humans lay at the center of creation. Logically, then, Earth must be the center of the universe. A theory that moved Earth—and all humankind—away from the center would be hard for the church's powerful leaders to accept. It would, in fact, change the way people understood their world.

So Copernicus kept fairly quiet about his ideas. He discussed them with a few friends and fellow mathematicians, but, for the most part, he just kept working away, reading and thinking and making notes, sometimes even in the margins of documents from his church job. He also began, very carefully, to calculate the movements of the planets, using his new model of the universe. If his calculations matched their actual movements, it would be a sign that he was on the right track.

THE ASTRONOMER IN THE TOWER

Just as I predicted!

In 1512, his uncle Lukas died, and Copernicus took a new job at nearby Frauenburg Cathedral, in northern Poland. He moved into a tower that was part of the town's walls and lived there for the rest of his life, serving the church during the day and studying the stars and planets in his spare time. He even built himself a special observation tower.

In 1514, Copernicus wrote a summary of his ideas, by hand, and showed it to a few friends. In it, he mentioned that he was working on a longer book, but years went by and the book didn't appear. Perhaps, like many scholars of the time, he felt no need to spread his ideas beyond that small circle of friends and fellow astronomers. Or perhaps he kept quiet because he knew his theory would cause a fuss. After all, Ptolemy's model of the universe, with Earth as its unmoving center, suited the Christian church just fine.

Still, word gradually spread among European astronomers that a minor church official in a distant part of Poland had come up with a revolutionary new idea. Many people who knew and respected Copernicus urged him to make his ideas more widely known, but—quietly and firmly—he resisted.

Finally, in 1539, when Copernicus was in his sixties, a young German professor of mathematics and astronomy, Rheticus, came to visit. And that changed everything.

COPERNICUS GOES PUBLIC

Rheticus had heard of Copernicus's skills as an astronomer and came to study with him. When the old man explained his sun-centered model of the universe, Rheticus was overwhelmed with excitement. He urged Copernicus to finish his book and publish it. Reluctantly, Copernicus agreed, and Rheticus began putting together the manuscript. It was a slow process in those days. For two years, Rheticus copied pages and pages of text and numbers by hand. Then he handed the manuscript over to a German Lutheran priest, Andreas Osiander, to turn into a printed book. That took another year.

Rheticus on trip #81 to Andreas's house

Copernicus was nervous. After all, he had spent his life in the service of the church. How would the church react? Osiander was nervous too. He wrote a short, unsigned preface—possibly without Copernicus's knowledge—saying that the idea of the planets circling the sun was just a convenient mathematical model, not necessarily a statement of fact. Still, everyone involved in the project knew the book would provoke a storm. And it did—eventually. In the end, however, Copernicus didn't have to face that storm.

A few months before the book was published, Copernicus suffered a stroke. On May 24, 1543, with the old man near death, a copy of *Concerning the Revolution of the Heavenly Spheres* reached Frauenburg, and his friends rushed it to his bedside. Weak and ill as he was, Copernicus was able to touch the book that held his life's work in astronomy. A few hours later, he died.

Aryabhata

A thousand years before Copernicus, a young Indian astronomer came up with the idea of a sun-centered system. Aryabhata was a brilliant mathematician. He calculated the distance around Earth—and came within 108 kilometers (67 miles) of the distance accepted today. In 499, when he was just 23 years old, Aryabhata wrote a book on math and astronomy, all in verse. In it, he explained that the stars appear to move across the sky because Earth is rotating on its own axis, and that Earth and the other planets revolve around the sun. He even realized that Earth's orbit isn't a perfect circle, as Copernicus thought, but an ellipse—a bit egg-shaped. Hindu religious leaders loathed Aryabhata's ideas, and even his admirers thought he couldn't possibly be right. Today, however, he's a hero in India, and the country's first satellite was named in his honor.

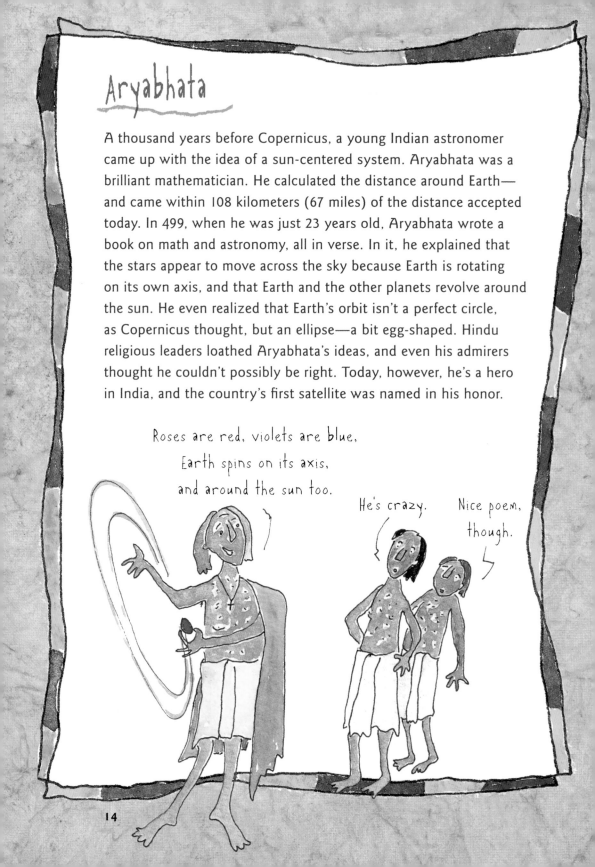

Roses are red, violets are blue,
Earth spins on its axis,
and around the sun too.

He's crazy.

Nice poem, though.

THE EARTH STARTS SPINNING

At first, there wasn't much fuss. Some churchmen condemned the book, but most people didn't really understand it. A few astronomers discussed Copernicus's ideas, but the church ignored them. Then, 90 years after Copernicus's death, the Italian scholar and professor Galileo Galilei was arrested and put on trial, just for writing about Copernicus's model of the universe.

Galileo hadn't been particularly interested in Copernicus's theory, although he had read the astronomer's book and found his mathematics convincing. All that changed when a Dutchman, Hans Lipperhey, invented the spyglass, which made faraway things appear closer. Galileo tinkered with the design and developed a more powerful instrument: the telescope. In January of 1610, he pointed his telescope at the night sky and saw what Copernicus had only been able to imagine.

The moon, through Galileo's telescope, was a huge, rough globe covered with mountains and craters, not smooth as astronomers had assumed. The Milky Way was thick with faint, distant stars invisible to the naked eye. The planets were distant, glowing globes floating in space, and one of them, Jupiter, even had four tiny moons circling it. Venus, he saw, had phases when part of the planet was lit and part was in shadow, just like our moon. Galileo realized that meant Venus was between Earth and the sun, and that he was seeing part or all of its shadowed side as it orbited the sun—just as Copernicus had described.

In fact, each detail his telescope revealed—from the moons of Jupiter to the phases of Venus—meshed with Copernicus's model of a sun-centered universe. Galileo was convinced that Copernicus was right. Church leaders warned him not to discuss Copernicus's ideas as fact, only as hypothesis, and Galileo tried to stay out of trouble. He wrote a book, *Dialogue Concerning the Two Chief World Systems*, published in 1632, which carefully presented both the Ptolemaic and the Copernican systems. However, he couldn't resist making it clear that the Copernican system made more sense.

In 1633, Galileo was arrested by church officials, put on trial, and convicted. He was forced, under the threat of torture, to swear an oath that his ideas about the shape of the universe were wrong. Then he was placed under house arrest at his home in Florence, and there he stayed for the rest of his life.

But it was too late. The ideas set out by Copernicus and confirmed by Galileo were loose in the world. More and more people discussed them and peered through telescopes to confirm them. Earth had lost its place at the center of the universe, and Copernicus had won.

Caroline Herschel and the Stars

Caroline Herschel was the most famous woman astronomer of her day. Born in Germany in 1750, she was tiny—just 1.3 meters (4 feet 3 inches) tall—as a result of a childhood illness. Her parents didn't expect much of her, but her favorite brother, William, did. When he got a job as a musician in England, he took Caroline along. She served as his housekeeper, while training as an opera singer and learning mathematics so she could help William with his hobby, astronomy. She became a well-known singer, but both William and Caroline made their marks as astronomers. They spent countless nights studying the stars through the powerful telescopes William built. Caroline kept the records and did the mathematical calculations that made sense of William's observations—including his discovery of the planet Uranus. Only when he was away did she get the telescope to herself, but she made good use of that time. Caroline Herschel discovered eight comets and several nebulae—great clouds of dust and gas found among the stars. She was the first woman to become an honorary member of Britain's Royal Astronomical Society, and on her 96th birthday, long after William's death, she was awarded the King of Prussia's Gold Medal for Science.

CHAPTER 2

SLIP-SLIDING AROUND THE WORLD

Copernicus may have set Earth in motion around the sun, but Alfred Wegener set the earth beneath our feet in motion. And his idea was no more welcome.

As solid as rock, we say. But rock isn't all that solid. Earthquakes shake and split the ground, volcanoes erupt, and landslides sweep away whole chunks of mountains. A century ago, Wegener, a young German scientist, proposed a theory that made rock seem even less solid. He said that entire continents move slowly across the face of the globe, dredging out oceans and pushing up mountains as they go. He called his idea "continental drift."

Geologists, scientists who specialize in rocks, didn't just doubt the idea. They hated it—partly because Wegener himself wasn't a geologist. What was he doing, dabbling in their corner of science? It didn't help that Wegener couldn't explain exactly why the continents moved, although he was sure that they did. And he was right.

MATCHING THE PUZZLE PIECES

It began, for Wegener, in 1910, when he looked at a map and realized how neatly the west coast of Africa would fit against the east coast of South America—almost as if they had been broken apart. He was fascinated, and decided to investigate. And when Wegener did something, he did it thoroughly.

52 hrs

He was 30 years old at the time, with a doctorate in astronomy and a career as a meteorologist, a scientist who studies weather patterns. He was also a bit of a daredevil. In 1906, he and his brother broke the world endurance record by staying up in a hot air balloon for more than 52 straight hours. The same year, he joined a Danish expedition to explore Greenland's northeast coast and study its weather patterns. There he had a glorious adventure, climbing ice cliffs, skiing across glaciers, and flying kites and small balloons high in the cold air to test the atmosphere.

Wonder where they pee in there.

He forgot to do the dishes before setting off.

Now he tackled his idea about the neatly fitting coastlines with the same enthusiasm. According to the accepted theory of the day, South America and Africa had once been joined by land. Then the land sank and the sea flowed in, creating the Atlantic Ocean. That explained one puzzle: researchers had been finding the same fossils and rock formations on both sides of the Atlantic.

However, Wegener noted, it didn't explain the matching coastlines. In fact, he found more places around the world where widely separated coastlines seemed to match.

The more he researched the problem, the more the world's continents looked like pieces of a single enormous jigsaw puzzle.

WEGENER GOES PUBLIC

On January 6, 1912, Wegener outlined his theory of continental drift to a group of geologists in Frankfurt. Earth's continents, he said, had once been one great continent, but it broke apart and the pieces were drifting slowly around the globe.

Where they moved apart, the oceans poured in and grew wider. Where they came together, they pushed up great mountain ranges.

His theory explained the coastlines, the matching fossils, and geological curiosities like a distinctive rock formation that appears in both Brazil and South Africa. And wandering continents would explain why the fossils of tropical plants and animals had been found locked in the rocks of islands in the Arctic.

None of that was enough to convince the geologists. They scoffed at the theory. What, after all, could a meteorologist know about continents? He was dabbling in science he didn't understand, they said.

Wegener was not an easy man to discourage. He was determined to find more evidence, but he was interrupted by another chance at adventure. He went back to his beloved Greenland and spent an entire winter camped on the ice cap, collecting data about the polar atmosphere.

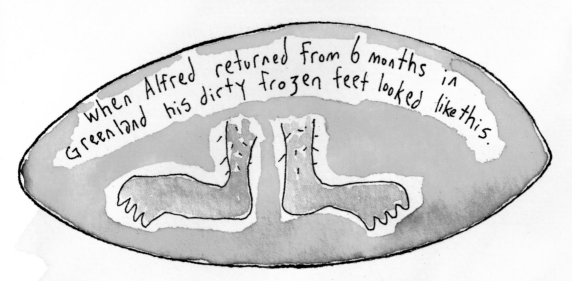

When Alfred returned from 6 months in Greenland his dirty frozen feet looked like this.

He and three colleagues traveled to their campsite and back on foot and ski, hauling all their supplies and scientific instruments in sleds. It was the longest trip across the Greenland ice cap ever made—another world record for Wegener.

Home in Germany, he continued to work as a meteorologist, tackling the research into continental drift in his spare time. He gathered evidence from many different branches of science, a radical approach at a time when most scientists stuck to their own fields. Wegener collected information about fossils, rock layers, mountain ranges, vegetation, and ancient weather patterns. If he didn't understand something, he tracked down an expert who could explain it. The evidence was coming together nicely.

Puzzling Over the Pieces

Alfred Wegener wasn't the first person to notice that the west coast of Africa and the east coast of South America looked like matching bits of a puzzle. The Flemish mapmaker Abraham Ortelius mentioned it in 1596. The Americas might have been torn away from Europe and Africa by earthquakes and floods, he said. In 1859, the French scientist Antonio Snider-Pellegrini also suggested that all the continents had once been joined together. He blamed their separation on the Great Flood described in the Bible. A few other people offered explanations for the matching coastlines over the years, but their ideas—like Wegener's—were generally dismissed as fanciful.

Young Earth, Old Earth

The processes that move whole continents are slow, so they only make sense if Earth is millions or billions of years old. In the 1700s, most people believed that Earth was only 6,000 years old. Biblical scholars had carefully counted back the years and generations in the Bible to come up with that number. James Hutton disagreed. Hutton spent years studying the structure of rocks on his farm in southern Scotland and came up with a new idea about the age of Earth. It was old—as he said, unknowably old. The rocks on his farm had been formed from layers of sediment laid down over millions or even hundreds of millions of years. Mountains and valleys, rock, soil, and sand had all formed slowly, and were still forming and changing. Hutton presented his theory in Edinburgh in 1785 and in a book published in 1788. Most people simply didn't believe him. But more than 30 years after Hutton's death, another geologist,

One million years, one million and one, one million and two . . .

Charles Lyell, rediscovered his ideas. By then, the evidence from geology and fossils had convinced most people that Earth was far older than 6,000 years. Lyell wrote about Hutton's ideas and the new evidence, and this time people believed.

THE THEORY GROWS

Wegener was getting ready to write a book about his theory when he was interrupted—again. In the summer of 1914, the First World War broke out in Europe, and Wegener was drafted into the German army. Within a few months, he had been wounded twice and was out of the fighting. Finally, while recovering in hospital, he could concentrate on his book.

Let's egg him!

His idea stinks.

He should stick with his storms.

PUZZLE OF THE WORLD

The Origin of Continents and Oceans was published in 1915. In it, Wegener wrote that about 300 million years ago, there had been one big continent, which he called *Pangaea* (from the Ancient Greek words meaning "entire Earth"). Bit by bit, Pangaea broke up. By 200 million years ago, the fragments were slowly drifting apart. He laid out his arguments and the evidence he had dug up, but German geologists still weren't convinced. One even called the theory "delirious ravings." But Wegener just kept digging.

Because it was wartime, the book wasn't published outside Germany. However, Wegener kept revising and republishing his book as he found more evidence. In 1923, long after the war was over, the third edition was published, translated into several languages, and distributed across Europe and beyond.

It didn't help. Geologists elsewhere in the world hated Wegener's theory just as much as German geologists had. He was accused of messing in things he didn't understand, and some scientists called his theory a fairy tale or geo-poetry. So much abuse was heaped on him that he couldn't get a university job in his home country, Germany. Perhaps the universities were afraid of controversy, or perhaps they objected to Wegener's tendency to stray beyond his own field of meteorology. Finally, a university in Austria hired him.

A SERIOUS GAP

HELP WANTED.

very old continent

Very old continent needs help moving. Would like new neighborhood with more night life and good restaurants. If you can help, please come to the south Pacific Ocean in the next 1,000 years.

Wegener kept defending his theory of continental drift, but he wasn't winning many converts. Part of the problem was that he couldn't explain what was making the continents move. He thought they were like great stone icebergs that plowed slowly through the heavier rock below, gouging out oceans and pushing up mountains. But what force could be strong enough to drive them? Maybe the rotation of Earth, Wegener suggested, or tides created by the sun and moon—but he wasn't satisfied with either explanation. Moreover, as others pointed out, rock can't plow through rock without breaking into pieces. It would be like forcing one piece of glass through an identical piece of glass. Something's bound to break. In fact, you're likely to have broken glass everywhere.

Despite these objections, Wegener was sure the continents were moving. He was simply prepared to leave some questions to be answered later, including the question of what made them move. He did, however, produce another edition of his book in 1929, answering many of his critics' questions. And then he left for Greenland one last time.

DEATH ON THE ICE

This time, the expedition's goal was to establish a winter weather station, but there were problems from the beginning. Ice blocked the harbor, and storms and cold kept the party from traveling. A small group made it to the location of the station, far inland, but the weather closed in again, cutting them off with few supplies. Worried about the men at the station, Wegener gathered a relief convoy of 15 dogsleds driven by himself, another meteorologist, and 13 experienced Greenlanders.

They set out, hauling tonnes of supplies, but the weather turned bad again. The wind howled and temperatures dropped as low as minus −54°C (−65°F). Most of the party turned back. Just the two meteorologists and one Greenlander slogged on through the cold. After five weeks, they finally reached the station and delivered the supplies that would see its staff through the winter. It was two days before Wegener's 50th birthday.

Wegener stayed just long enough to celebrate his birthday with his friends.

But you're two days early for your surprise party.

Boy, are we glad to see you!

-65°F

HAPPY 50th BIRTHDAY FRED!

Then he and the young Greenlander, Rasmus Villumsen, started back toward the coast. They were never seen alive again. The next spring, searchers found Wegener's frozen body, laid out respectfully on a reindeer hide and sleeping bag and buried in the snow. Villumsen was never found.

THE FORCE IS FOUND

At the time of Wegener's death, his theory was still considered fictional nonsense by most of the scientific world. Geology students were warned that talking about continental drift could put an end to their academic careers. It would take another 30 years, and some new tools, before his idea of continental drift was confirmed. In the 1950s and early 1960s, scientists used sound waves to map the sea floor, where molten rock welled up from cracks in the seabed. They measured the magnetism of rocks to see how they had moved over Earth's surface or tracked tiny changes in the distance between continents with radar. The new evidence showed that Wegener was right: the continents do indeed move. They don't plough through rock, as he had imagined. Instead they are part of great plates that make up the outer crust of Earth and float on the hot rock beneath.

The theory is now called plate tectonics, but Wegener's idea of continental drift is part of it. The man dismissed as a teller of geological fairy tales is now a hero of modern geology. If he hadn't died on that Greenland ice cap, he might even have lived long enough to enjoy the recognition.

Marie Tharp and the Undersea Valley

The American mapmaker Marie Tharp provided the missing link that explained Alfred Wegener's moving continents— but it took months to get her colleagues to pay attention.

Born in 1920, Tharp first studied arts at university, but switched to geology during the Second World War. Women didn't normally take geology then, but many young men had left to fight in the war, and the oil industry needed geologists.

Tharp got graduate degrees in both geology and math. Then—after the war—she went to work for a scientist who was using sound waves to map the ocean floor. While the men of the team worked on the survey ship, she was back at the office, drawing maps based on the information they collected. In 1952, while she was mapping mountains beneath the Atlantic Ocean, she spotted a cleft that seemed to run the length of the mountain range. It looked like a rift valley, she thought—a land formation created when Earth's surface pulls apart. If it was a rift valley, it could mean that the crust beneath the ocean was pulling apart, the ocean was widening, and Wegener had been right about continental drift. She pointed it out to her colleagues, but they still thought continental drift was a crazy idea. While they argued, she kept on mapping.

Eight months after she first suggested the idea, her closest colleague, Bruce Heezen, admitted she was right. The maps the two of them developed and published over the next 20 years were vital to the new science of plate tectonics, which built on Wegener's ideas.

CHAPTER 3

WASH YOUR HANDS!

Today, everybody knows about germs. Even four-year-olds will tell you, as they wash their hands, that germs make you sick. But that's fairly new knowledge—barely 150 years old.

For most of human history, no one even knew germs existed. After all, they are far too small to see without a microscope. Even when Antoni van Leeuwenhoek looked through his newly constructed microscope in 1677 and discovered tiny organisms in a drop of water, he didn't connect them with disease. How could something so small sicken something as large as a human being?

There were plenty of other explanations for disease, from overeating to the movements of the stars and planets. From the Middle Ages until late in the 19th century, many people, including doctors, thought disease was spread by miasmas— poisonous, evil-smelling vapors that carried bits of decaying material through the air. During that time, there were plenty of evil smells, especially in cities. Sewage often flowed in open channels down the streets, garbage rotted in alleys, and the horses used for transportation left plenty of droppings behind.

Look out!
Miasma
overhead.

Germs observed
in the Middle Ages

Wealthy people used perfumes to cover bad smells or sometimes cleaned up the source of the smell. Perfumes were no
protection from disease, we now know, but if the smell came
from germy things like sewage or rotting garbage, cleaning
up the source actually did help.

A few people, however, were beginning to suspect that
disease might be spread another way. For some illnesses, none
of the traditional explanations made sense—especially in the
case of puerperal fever, also known as childbed fever.

Miasma Wins in Italy

In the 1850s, the Italian anatomist Filippo Pacini discovered the bacterium, or germ, that causes cholera. Cholera is a highly contagious disease that still kills today, especially in places where water is contaminated with sewage. Pacini not only found the bacterium, but wrote several papers about it and even suggested ways to treat the disease. That was three decades before the German scientist Robert Koch made the same discovery. Despite all Pacini's work, his findings were utterly ignored. The problem was that Italian doctors still believed in the miasma theory, that diseases spread through vapors in the air. They weren't prepared to listen to anything that didn't fit that theory.

MEDICAL MYSTERY

Childbed fever was a horrible sickness that killed new mothers and their babies. The mother might be strong and healthy when her baby was born. Then, a few days after the birth, she would start suffering chills and fever. After days of fever and pain, she either recovered or, all too often, died. Sometimes the babies sickened and died too.

Doctors and midwives who helped with the births were baffled. The illness could sweep through a hospital or a town and then fade away, but no one could pinpoint a cause or a common thread in the outbreaks. For pregnant women caught up in one of the outbreaks, it was terrifying.

Then, in 1847, a Hungarian doctor working in Austria lost a friend—and gained an idea.

A TALE OF TWO CLINICS

Ignaz Philipp Semmelweis grew up in Buda, Hungary, and moved to Vienna in 1837, when he was 19, to go to university. He studied medicine, specializing in medicine related to child-birth. In 1846, he got a job supervising one of the maternity clinics at Vienna General Hospital, where doctors and midwives (specialists in helping with childbirth) were trained. Semmelweis was in charge of First Clinic, where the medical students were trained. Midwives were trained in Second Clinic.

First Clinic, Semmelweis soon realized, had a problem. Women and babies were dying from childbed fever in First Clinic—far too many of them. The death rate for women and newborn babies in Semmelweis's clinic was more than 13 percent.

In Second Clinic, where the student midwives worked, the death rate was barely over 2 percent. Word of the high death rate in First Clinic had spread, and women coming to the hospital to give birth often begged tearfully to be assigned to the midwives' clinic.

CLINIC #1

CLINIC #2
98%
SATISFACTION

I want Clinic 2!

Me too!

those corpse bits again

cut

scalpel with icky
corpse bits

dead doctor

A SIMPLE ACCIDENT

Semmelweis tried, without success, to figure out why so
many women in First Clinic were dying, and why the results
in Second Clinic were so different. Then, in March 1847,
he returned from a holiday in Venice to find that another
doctor, a good friend, had died.

The doctor had been supervising an autopsy on a patient
who had died of childbed fever. The students and doctors of
First Clinic regularly dissected the corpses of dead patients,
both to learn about diseases and to figure out what had killed
the patient. One of the medical students who was involved in
this particular autopsy had accidentally pricked the doctor's
finger with his dissecting knife. Within days, Semmelweis's
friend fell ill and died.

When the grieving Semmelweis read the description of his friend's symptoms, he realized that they were exactly like the symptoms of the women dying of childbed fever. The cut finger was the clue he'd been looking for. The doctor had died after the open wound in his finger came in contact with the dead body. That, Semmelweis concluded, must be the way the disease was transmitted.

SEMMELWEIS FOLLOWS HIS NOSE

In those days, doctors rarely washed their hands before moving from one patient to another. In First Clinic, where they worked in the morgue as well, both the doctors and students might go from dissecting a patient dead of childbed fever straight to examining a woman in the middle of giving birth, all without washing their hands or changing their stained clothes.

Semmelweis concluded that bits of what he called "cadaverous material" were stuck to the hands of doctors and medical students and passed on to the women and babies around the time of birth. In Second Clinic, where the midwife students didn't dissect corpses and so didn't come in contact with the cadaverous material, there were far fewer chances for the disease to spread.

Today, Semmelweis's conclusion seems obvious because we know so much more about how germs spread. But until the late 1800s, most doctors simply didn't realize their dirty hands and clothes were hurting their patients. Semmelweis, however, followed the evidence of his nose. He could smell the stink of corpses on the hands of students and doctors coming into the clinic from the morgue.

"Wash!" he said.

In fact, he went further. Semmelweis ordered everyone—doctors, students, midwives—to wash their hands with diluted bleach before they visited a patient. In addition, he had the wards regularly washed down with a cleaning solution. Many people, especially the doctors, weren't happy about it, but Semmelweis insisted. The result was that the death rate from childbed fever dropped to nearly zero in both clinics within two years.

Alexander Gordon of Aberdeen

Fifty years before Semmelweis ordered health workers in Vienna to clean up their act, a Scottish doctor named Alexander Gordon figured out that dirty hands spread childbed fever. Formerly a surgeon in the Royal Navy, Gordon was working in Aberdeen as a midwife and physician in 1792 when there was a serious outbreak of the fever. Gordon didn't know what caused it, but he noticed a pattern. If a woman was helped by a nurse or midwife who had been with a sick woman, the second woman fell ill a couple of days later. He realized that the sickness must somehow be carried on the attendants' hands or clothes. The clothes and bedclothes of sick patients should be purified or burned, he wrote in a short brochure, and medical workers should wash thoroughly and fumigate their clothes before moving on to new patients. Gordon himself treated 77 patients during the outbreak, and 25 died. He was horrified to realize that he might well have caused some of the deaths. Gordon might have written more about preventing childbed fever, but he was called back to the Royal Navy, where he developed tuberculosis. He died in 1799, just 47 years old.

Keep those bedsheets coming!

Off with the aprons, ladies!

SAINT HELENS HOSPITAL

BACK TO HUNGARY

Semmelweis kept careful track of the death rates in the two clinics. He experimented with different approaches to cleaning, and he added procedures when he found that disease had apparently been transmitted between patients as well as from the dead. The one thing he didn't do was let the world know about his findings—either through public talks or written papers.

He might have worried that his German wasn't good enough, or he might have thought the record of the two clinics spoke for itself. Whatever the reason, that failure came back to haunt him.

Semmelweis's procedures saved lives, but they made enemies. The clinic staff thought the time-consuming washing was unnecessary, and senior doctors were offended by the idea that they had been harming their patients. Even Semmelweis's careful records, showing the decline in deaths, weren't enough. It didn't help that Semmelweis couldn't explain, in scientific terms, why handwashing worked. He just knew that it did. In 1849, he was fired by his supervisor, one of the senior doctors he had offended.

Soon after, he moved back to Hungary.

Back home, Semmelweis found another job in a maternity hospital and continued to promote handwashing and cleaning to keep disease down. He had the same kind of success in lowering the death rate in the Hungarian hospital, but no more success in convincing the world that his methods were the right approach. The Hungarian staff considered them a nuisance, and the rest of Europe paid little attention to Hungary, so news of his work went nowhere.

Finally, in 1861, Semmelweis published a book about his findings and methods, 14 years after the experience in Vienna. Unfortunately, the book was more than 500 pages long, badly written, and almost unreadable. Whole chunks were devoted to attacking his critics rather than explaining his methods.

He even wrote angry letters to the doctors who wouldn't follow his methods, accusing some of murder. And still Semmelweis couldn't explain exactly how material from the dead bodies killed mothers and babies. Not surprisingly, few people read the book and even fewer were convinced by it.

A SAD END

Semmelweis grew more and more bitter—and more and more odd. He had always been sensitive to criticism, even before his book appeared. After it came out, he alternately raged against his critics and fell into bouts of despair. Finally, in 1865, his friends and family committed him to a sanatorium, a kind of hospital for the mentally ill.

In those days, people with mental illnesses were often treated badly. They might be chained, caged, or kept in straitjackets, and bathed or fed by force. We don't know how Semmelweis was treated, but two weeks after he entered the sanatorium, he was dead. There are several stories about what killed him.

One blames a beating by one of the attendants. Another blames a cut finger, leading to massive infection—just like the infection that killed his friend in Vienna so many years earlier.

Almost immediately, Semmelweis and his accomplishments were forgotten, both in Vienna and in his home country of Hungary. Then, in the last third of the 1800s, the French chemist Louis Pasteur made the connection between the tiny organisms he saw through his microscope and diseases. Soon after that, an English surgeon named Joseph Lister introduced the idea of sterilizing wounds and surgical instruments, and a German scientist, Robert Koch, identified the specific organisms that caused some illnesses. That was the beginning of our understanding of germs.

And finally, the medical world rediscovered accounts of Semmelweis's work in Vienna. A biography written in 1909, long after his death, painted a picture of him as a hero, fighting for the health of mothers and babies—and driven to madness by the opposition he faced. Although that's probably as much fiction as fact, Semmelweis is now considered an important figure in the history of medicine.

Germ heroes of the past

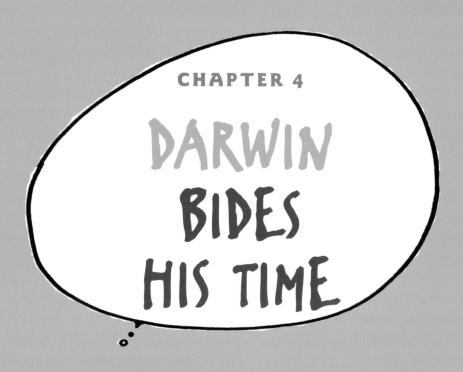

CHAPTER 4

DARWIN BIDES HIS TIME

Ideas that make us rethink how we fit into the universe or even into the world around us are hard to sell. Copernicus knew that, and Alfred Wegener learned it. A century and a half after Charles Darwin's book on evolution, *The Origin of Species*, was published, some people are still struggling with its ideas and how they fit with religious stories of creation.

When Darwin made his theory public, there were plenty of doubters. The idea that plants and animals—all life, in fact—had developed and changed into new forms and species over thousands and millions of years was difficult to accept. After all, many people still believed that Earth was just a few thousand years old and all animals and plants had been created by God just as we see them today. Even those who accepted the idea of an older Earth found it hard to believe that such a long, slow process had created the diversity of life they saw around them.

Darwin's ideas were criticized and ridiculed by many people. If he had published his theory when he first figured it out, however, things might have been much worse. He might have met the kind of firestorm that greeted Galileo, or he might have been forgotten, like James Hutton and Ignaz Semmelweis. But Darwin was patient. He waited years, establishing his scientific reputation and building his arguments and evidence. When he finally announced his theory to the world, he was wealthy, middle-aged, and a respected scientist.

It all started out quite differently.

This is how we all remember Darwin, but . . .

Once upon a time he was small and loved to collect beetles.

Well, Fitzroy, this should be a jolly good adventure!

BEE-GUL
BEAGLE

DARWIN'S GREAT ADVENTURE

We usually see pictures of Charles Darwin in his last years, with a long, white beard. That's not the Charles Darwin who sailed away on the survey ship HMS *Beagle* in 1831. Then he was just 22 years old, a young English gentleman in search of adventure. Fresh out of university, Darwin was in no hurry to get serious about life. He wanted to travel.

The offer to join the *Beagle* on its five-year voyage to map the coastlines of South America was perfect, and Darwin talked his wealthy father into letting him go. His main job was to be a companion to the captain, Robert Fitzroy, who was only a few years older than Darwin. A captain couldn't socialize with the crew in those class-conscious days, so he often took along a gentleman passenger as company. When Darwin wasn't occupied with the captain, he was free to pursue his own interests as a naturalist, and his work turned out to be an important part of HMS *Beagle*'s scientific mission.

What is a species?

When Darwin was sailing the world, the definition of *species* was fairly simple. It meant a group of animals that can interbreed. Appearance isn't enough to identify species. For example, all dogs—from Chihuahuas to Saint Bernards—are considered a single species, whereas three nearly identical mockingbirds can come from three different species. Now things are getting more complicated. Genetic analysis gives us a whole new way to see how animals and plants are related, and the results don't always match our expectations. Some species can breed with other species. Captive male lions and female tigers, for example, have occasionally crossbred. Their offspring, called *ligers*, are the largest cats in the world. Grizzly bears and polar bears in the wild have produced a few half-and-half cubs called *grolar bears*. In other cases, animals that look identical turn out to be quite different genetically and don't interbreed. Today, if you ask scientists in three different fields to define *species*, you'll likely get three different answers. So, what is a species? Keep your eye on the science news for the latest!

Darwin came prepared. He hauled along whole trunks full of scientific books and equipment. He was no beginner at science; his favorite pastime in England had been roaming the fields to collect and classify beetles. Now he was curious to see what species of plants and animals he might find in foreign fields.

Some of Darwin's luggage for the trip

YEAR #1 ON BEAGLE

YEAR #3

YEAR #5

SLOTH BONES
TO BIRD BEAKS

The trip began badly. As soon as the
Beagle set sail, Darwin got horribly seasick—
and he never really overcame his seasickness
during the entire five-year voyage. But once
he reached shore, he was tireless. He tramped
up mountainsides to examine exposed rock
layers, he scoured hillsides for fossils, and
he picked over forests and fields in search
of new or interesting plants and animals.

The *Beagle* crossed the Atlantic and sailed
down the coast of South America, looping
around its southern tip, and back up the
continent's west coast. In September 1835,
the *Beagle* crossed to the tiny Galápagos
Islands, isolated in the Pacific Ocean.
It spent five weeks charting and exploring
the island group before sailing on westward.
Eventually, the little ship circled the globe.

The stop in Galápagos was life-changing
for Darwin, but he didn't know it at the
time. Just as he had elsewhere, he roamed
the islands, collecting samples, preserving
specimens, and taking pages upon pages of
notes. By October 2, 1836, when the *Beagle*
reached England and Darwin walked down

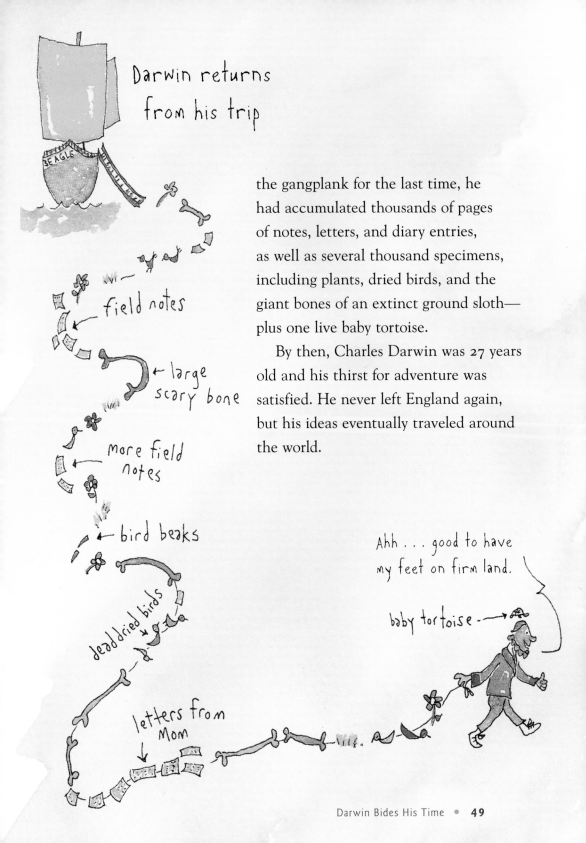

Darwin returns from his trip

field notes

← large scary bone

more field notes

← bird beaks

dead dried birds

letters from Mom
↓

Ahh . . . good to have my feet on firm land.

baby tortoise →

the gangplank for the last time, he had accumulated thousands of pages of notes, letters, and diary entries, as well as several thousand specimens, including plants, dried birds, and the giant bones of an extinct ground sloth— plus one live baby tortoise.

By then, Charles Darwin was 27 years old and his thirst for adventure was satisfied. He never left England again, but his ideas eventually traveled around the world.

Mary Anning and the Bones

In the 19th century, fossils were popular objects to collect and study, and that helped people accept the idea that Earth is very ancient. It's possible that no one in early 19th-century England knew more about fossils than Mary Anning. We'll never know for sure, since she didn't write books or make speeches; she was a professional fossil collector. Born in 1799, Anning lived in the seaside resort of Lyme Regis. Her family was desperately poor, and she started working at the age of 11. She and her brother and mother scoured the eroding cliffs near their home and sold the fossils they found from a table outside their tiny cottage. At the age of 12, Anning brought home the world's first fossil ichthyosaur, an ancient dolphin-like marine reptile. Later she discovered the first plesiosaur (a long-necked marine reptile) and Britain's first pterosaur (a flying reptile). Anning read everything she could find about fossils, sometimes copying entire articles, with their illustrations, by hand. The wealthy scientists who bought her fossils stayed to discuss them with her, recognizing her expertise, but it was the male scientists who were credited with the scientific discoveries, not Anning. At that time, science was largely restricted to well-off men, and Anning was both a woman and poor.

Still, after her death in 1847, the president of the Royal Geological Society delivered a speech in her honor. More than a century later, scientists from around the world attended a four-day event to celebrate the 200th anniversary of Mary Anning's birth.

plesiosaur 10p
fossil
lemonade 5p

THE SLOW GROWTH OF A DARING IDEA

Darwin's first chore at home in England was to study all
the specimens and notes he had brought back and write articles
about what he had discovered. The first articles, some sent
home while he was still traveling, were mostly about geology.
He worked hard, and very soon he had established himself
as a respected geologist.

But as he studied some of his biological specimens, Darwin
got the beginning of an idea. The birds he had collected on
the Galápagos Islands were the key. Among them were some
small birds with beaks in a variety of shapes and sizes. Darwin
assumed that they belonged to several different species.

To his surprise, a bird expert identified them all as finches—even though some had narrow beaks for catching insects, some had heavy, seed-cracking beaks, and some even had parrot-like beaks for picking buds and fruit. The expert also identified three previously unknown species of mockingbird, collected from three different islands in the Galápagos chain.

Darwin began to wonder if the birds might come from common ancestors that had reached the islands long ago, and if they might have changed over time to suit the conditions and food found on their particular islands.

That was the beginning of his theory of evolution by natural selection. Essentially, it said that species evolve over many generations because only the animals or plants best adapted to their habitat survive to reproduce. If a flock of finches arrives on an island where the best food source is seeds, the birds with slightly stronger seed-cracking beaks will flourish and produce chicks. Over generations, more and more of the island's finches will inherit big beaks from their big-beaked parents, until gradually the beaks of all the island's finches are strong seed-crackers. The result can be the evolution of a brand new species.

Darwin's Rejected Finch Theories

This finch always had its mouth open to catch flies.

This finch ate curly worms.

This finch dined primarily on branches.

DARWIN PLAYS IT SMART

Darwin wrote his ideas down in secret notebooks. By about 1838, he said later, his theory was fully thought out. However, he didn't write an article for publication. In fact, he told only a few close friends about it. Why?

One reason was that he was known as a geologist, not a biologist. He needed to establish his reputation in biology before other biologists would believe him. Secondly, he knew his ideas would cause a fuss in the scientific world. Unless he had solid evidence, and plenty of it, the ideas would be rejected. A few odd birds from some remote islands would not be enough to convince the skeptics.

Finally, he knew that the idea of evolution would upset religious people, as it still does sometimes. Darwin's wife Emma, whom he loved dearly, was very religious—and so he waited and thought and built up his evidence before upsetting her and the rest of society.

Long Legs and Muscles

The French naturalist Jean-Baptiste Lamarck tried to explain the kind of changes Darwin saw, but his explanation didn't work. In 1801, he suggested an individual animal's actions could change the shape of its body, and that those changes might be passed on to the next generation. For example, the long legs of wading birds might have developed because the birds stretched upward to keep their bodies dry, and parent birds passed on long-leggedness to their chicks. Eventually, all wading birds had long legs. Unfortunately for Lamarck, there was no evidence nature worked that way, and considerable evidence that it didn't. After all, your mother or grandfather might have big muscles from lifting weights, but that doesn't mean you were born with big muscles and weight-lifting skills. By the time Darwin came along, most people had abandoned Lamarck's ideas.

THE RUSH TO PUBLISH

Twenty years later, Darwin was still hesitating, still building his case. The book was largely written, he had established his credentials as a biologist, and he had collected lots of evidence from massive studies on barnacles and orchids, as well as breeding experiments with pigeons. But it was never quite enough. Darwin was a perfectionist.

Then he received a paper from a young biologist, Alfred Russel Wallace, who had reached much the same conclusions as Darwin about evolution. Wallace had also traveled to South America and had seen many of the things Darwin saw on the voyage of the *Beagle*. Darwin was stuck. He couldn't ignore Wallace's paper, but he didn't want to lose the recognition of his own years of work.

So, with Wallace's agreement, Darwin prepared a short version of his own theory and arranged for both his and Wallace's papers to be published together.

Then he finally completed his masterwork, *The Origin of Species*, and published it. It appeared in bookstores in late 1859, almost 25 years after his brief time on the Galápagos Islands.

Just as Darwin had expected, the book caused a fuss. The first print run of 1,250 copies sold out on the first day. Both scientists and religious leaders attacked it, and Darwin's friends defended it, helped by the massive amount of detail and careful argument Darwin had assembled over a quarter of a century.

Darwin himself, once an adventurous young man, stayed quietly in his country home with his family and took little part in the arguments. He continued to tinker and revise and improve his theory until his death in 1882. Since then, more and more scientific evidence has confirmed Darwin's theory and added to it. Today, we can even reconstruct the process of a species' evolution in its genes.

A Publishing and Evolutionary Sensation

The evolution best seller of the 19th century wasn't written by Darwin. It was a popular science book called *Vestiges of the Natural History of Creation*, published anonymously in 1844. It sold thousands of copies and was reprinted at least a dozen times. Among its fans were future American president Abraham Lincoln, Queen Victoria, and the poet Tennyson. The author, revealed well after his death, was Robert Chambers, a Scottish journalist and publisher. He wasn't a scientist, but he was a good writer who mashed together bits of astronomy, geology, and biology, along with speculation about evolution. His idea was that life evolved from primitive animals, such as fish, through higher animals, such as mammals, with humans as evolution's goal and crowning achievement. (Actually, white, European men were at the top of Chambers's evolutionary ladder.) The theory appealed to progress-minded Victorians, but it didn't take long for scientists to point out serious mistakes in the science and for non-scientists to express horror at the idea that they might be descended from animals. Also, Chambers couldn't explain why living things evolved. However, the popularity of the book meant that 15 years later, when Darwin published his theory of natural selection, people were already used to discussions about evolution.

CHAPTER 5

SOAR LIKE AN EAGLE, LAND LIKE A ROCK

People have probably dreamed about flying since the first time someone looked up and watched a bird soar through the air. However, actually getting off the ground—and getting back down safely—has taken a while. The delay wasn't due to lack of desire. It just took time to develop the right kind of technology.

The first successful powered flight took place in 1903, when an American, Orville Wright, climbed into the airplane he and his brother Wilbur had built and took to the air for 12 long seconds. The brothers had been working toward powered flight for several years by then, but they didn't start from scratch. They had dug out all the previous research they could find about flying. That's how they found out about Sir George Cayley.

THE BOY FROM PARADISE

Cayley was born in 1773 and grew up on his wealthy family's northern England estate, in a district called Paradise. When he was about 20, Cayley saw the design of a toy helicopter that had been demonstrated in Paris in 1784. It was essentially two propellers made from bird feathers and powered by a twisted string, but it had worked. Cayley designed his own version of the helicopter toy, but quickly became more interested in a different kind of flight. He wanted to build something that would fly like a bird, on wings.

Well, not exactly like a bird. That was one of Cayley's most important contributions to the science of flight. People were already taking to the air when he began his work, but by floating in balloons, which are lighter than air. Cayley was interested in how something heavier than air, such as a bird, could fly. He analyzed bird flight and broke the process down into individual components. Essentially, each of these components was a problem that had to be solved in order to get a heavier-than-air object into the sky. Birds had solved all of the problems, but their solutions might not be the only ones.

George has another nice toy . . .

SOAR LIKE A SEAGULL

People had already tried to build flying contraptions with flapping, birdlike wings, and it hadn't worked. Cayley realized that flapping wasn't actually necessary. Seagulls could soar for ages with their wings outstretched and barely moving, controlling their flight by slight adjustments to the angle and shape of their wings.

Successful flight, he concluded, depended on lift (the force that causes a wing to rise when air flows past it quickly), propulsion (the force that moves the bird, or plane, forward), and control (the ability to steer the flight). Breaking the problem down allowed him to tackle the components of flight separately.

Cayley didn't waste time. In 1799, he engraved his first known airplane design on a small silver disc that is now in the Science Museum in London, England. It shows the effect of breaking flight into parts. There's a curved, sail-like wing arching over a boat-shaped pilot's compartment. That would provide lift. For propulsion, a flapper sticks out behind the compartment, presumably operated by pilot muscle power. Control came from a long-handled rudder attached to vanes that would push against the air.

Lift, propulsion, control!
Lift, propulsion, control!

Cayley had just 3 things on his mind much of the time.

Other well-fed trout plane designs by Cayley

Cayley didn't actually build the plane he sketched. Instead he tinkered with other designs and experimented with wing shapes. In 1804, he built a glider, with a fixed wing and a tail much like a modern airplane's, to test his solutions for lift and control. It was a fragile thing made of bamboo and cloth, but it flew, if only about the length of a basketball court. Then he carried on experimenting and tinkering for another five years. Cayley even figured out the best streamlined shape to reduce air resistance—based, he explained, on the shape of a well-fed trout. So, when you look at an airplane, think fish!

WRAPPING IT UP, FOR A WHILE

In 1809, Cayley published three articles that laid out the principles of heavier-than-air flight and described all he'd learned over the past decade of thought and experiment. He also wrote about the problem he hadn't been able to solve: propulsion.

The most powerful kind of engine available in 1809 was the steam engine. However, everything about steam engines was heavy: thick metal, coal or wood fuel, and water.

Maybe someday . . .

Cayley couldn't find or design a steam engine light enough for an airplane. He had tried a few other engine ideas—including a hot air engine and an engine that used gunpowder to fire its pistons—but they were no more successful. In fact, the gunpowder engine was downright dangerous and more likely to blow the airplane up than drive it forward.

The propulsion problem defeated Cayley, but not forever. He was perfectly confident, he wrote, that people would soon be able to travel by air more safely than by water. He predicted that the marvelous airplanes of the future would travel at blinding speeds, as fast as 160 kilometers (100 miles) an hour.

Spain's flying Moors

There are several variations of the story of the flying Moors, dating from the time when the Moors (North African Muslims) ruled much of Spain. All were written down much later, so it's hard to know what really happened. Here's one version. Armen Firman tried flying first, around 852 CE, using a cloak-like garment stiffened with wooden rods. He didn't exactly fly, but the cloak slowed his fall enough that he escaped with only minor injuries. The scholar, poet, and inventor Abbas Ibn Firnas saw Firman's attempted flight and, in 875 CE, he built his own glider. The flight went well, but the landing didn't, and he hurt his back badly. While no reports from the time survive, a line of poetry does. Written by a poet who didn't much like Ibn Firnas, it says: "He flew faster than the phoenix in his flight when he dressed his body in the feathers of a vulture."

The Flying Monk

Eilmer of Malmesbury was an English monk, born late in the 10th century. When he was still a young man, he built himself a flying contraption, probably in the form of wings strapped to his body. He launched himself, according to legend, from the abbey roof and glided about the length of two football fields before crashing and breaking both his legs. After that, the abbot strictly forbade any more flying experiments. Eilmer lived a long life, although he limped badly. He apparently felt he'd gone wrong by failing to include a tail in his contraption.

It seemed like a good idea yesterday

CAYLEY RETURNS TO THE AIR

After publishing his 1809 articles, Cayley put aside airplanes to work on other things. Among his inventions: an artificial hand (designed for a local boy who had lost his hand), a self-righting lifeboat, a caterpillar tractor, and improved brakes for railway trains.

Then, in 1842, he plunged right back into aeronautics. The trigger was a scheme proposed by William Henson and John Stringfellow, engineers working on lacemaking machinery. The lacemaking business had hit hard times, so Henson came up with an idea. He and Stringfellow would build an amazing airplane, the Aerial Steam Carriage, and start transporting people by air from city to city, he said.

FLY THE AMAZING AERIAL STEAM CARRIAGE

Henson, all we need is that first customer to get things rolling . . .

FULL REFUND IF YOUR FLIGHT CRASHES

They had never built an airplane, or anything like it, but that didn't discourage Henson. To attract investors, and perhaps to give the impression he knew what he was doing, Henson claimed to be following in the footsteps of Sir George Cayley, "the Father of Aerial Navigation."

Cayley took one look at the blueprints and knew the airplane wouldn't work. Its wingspan would stretch almost from end to end of an Olympic swimming pool, and it would weigh about as much as six big grizzly bears. The power came from a huge, heavy steam engine. Cayley realized the airplane would fly like a rock, straight into the ground.

In 1843, Cayley wrote a paper that laid out exactly what was wrong with Henson's design. He was right, and Henson and Stringfellow's grand scheme slowly faded away, but the 70-year-old Cayley's enthusiasm for aviation came bounding back, fresh as ever.

The Power of Rubber Bands

If you've ever flown a toy airplane powered by a rubber band, you're in good company. The Frenchman Alphonse Pénaud was the first person to build and fly heavier-than-air model flying machines powered by rubber bands. In August 1871, one of his models flew 55 meters (181 feet) in 11 seconds. Pénaud's models weren't toys. They were experiments intended to help him design full-size airplanes. In 1876, he and his partner, Paul Gauchot, developed a proposal for a large, single-winged airplane with retractable landing gear and a number of other modern-looking features, but when they tried to get funding to build it, no one listened. Pénaud, who was just 30 years old, was so upset that his machine would never be built that he killed himself.

THE BOY-CARRIER AND THE MAN-CARRIER

Cayley started experimenting with entirely new designs for gliders. He came up with the idea of stacking wings two or three high, an idea the Wright brothers later used for the biplane that carried Orville on his first flight. In 1849, Cayley tested a glider with three stacked wings (a triplane). It was pulled into the air like a kite by several people hauling on a rope. He called it his "boy-carrier" because a 10-year-old boy from his estate was aboard. The glider left the ground and floated for several meters before settling back to earth.

Finally, there was Cayley's man-carrier. When his grand-daughter Dora was an old lady, she described a test flight she had witnessed around 1853, when she was nine years old. According to the story, Cayley, then 80 years old, had built a glider big enough to carry a man, and somehow he talked his coachman into acting as passenger.

A group of men lined up along the ropes attached to the glider and hauled it faster and faster down a slope until it took to the air and sailed about twice the length of a football field—while the terrified coachman hung on with all his might—before crash-landing in a field. According to Dora, the poor coachman scrambled out of the machine and announced, "Please, Sir George, I wish to give notice. I was hired to drive and not to fly!"

Now, Cayley's plans say the propeller goes at the front.

The Wright brothers' first plane

CAYLEY LIVES ON

After Cayley died in 1857, his son Digby, who found the whole aeronautics obsession embarrassing, locked his father's notes and diaries away. For a while, Cayley was almost forgotten. But not entirely. The Wright brothers found copies of Cayley's 1809 articles, and there they discovered most of the basic information they needed to design their plane. They built themselves the one thing Cayley had lacked: a lightweight, powerful engine. It was a version of the gas-powered internal combustion engine, which had been developed around the time of Cayley's death. It was, in fact, just the sort of engine Cayley had dreamed about almost a century earlier.

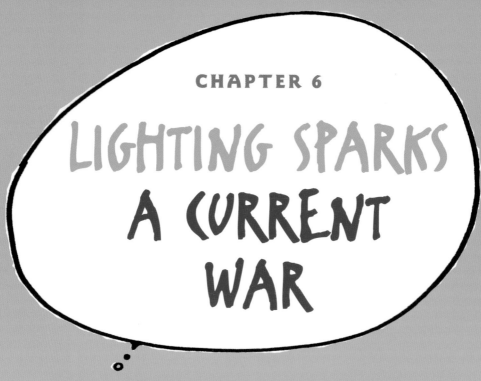

CHAPTER 6

LIGHTING SPARKS A CURRENT WAR

Nikola Tesla was a brilliant inventor, bursting with nifty ideas about electricity and what it could do. Some of them were truly ahead of his time. Even now, 70 years after his death, some of them look like pie in the sky. But don't dismiss them. A lot of his wild ideas have come true.

Tesla's greatest success, however, is something so common that we don't even think about it. When you walk into a dark room and flick the switch to turn on the lights, you're using Tesla's legacy: alternating current electricity.

There are two main kinds of electrical current: alternating current (AC) and direct current (DC). In AC, the direction of flow switches back and forth. In DC, it flows in one direction. When you plug a lamp into a wall socket, you're using AC. When you put batteries in your flashlight, you're using DC.

Both kinds of current have advantages and disadvantages. In the 1880s and 1890s, when electricity was beginning to be

used for big things like lighting cities and running machinery, electrical companies fought over which kind of electricity to use. Tesla, a passionate supporter of AC, was in the thick of the battle, and his side won.

But, in many ways, Tesla lost the war. He was a brilliant inventor, but a terrible businessman—and Tesla's dreams were very big business indeed.

A PASSION FOR ELECTRICITY

When he was three years old, in what is now Croatia,
Nikola Tesla stroked the family cat and raised a small
shower of sparks. Startled, he asked his father what it was.
"Just electricity," his father said, and explained that lightning
was electricity too, but on a bigger scale. From that time on,
Tesla was obsessed with electricity.

Wow,
I think
I'm onto
something...

The trouble was, he was supposed
to become a priest. In Tesla's rather
respectable family, boys became
army officers or priests, not electrical
engineers. A battle between father
and son was brewing until the teenage
Nikola fell desperately ill with cholera.
From his sickbed, Nikola made his
father promise that, if he survived, he
could become an electrical engineer.
His father agreed, and Nikola's future
was settled.

While studying electrical engineering, Tesla became
fascinated by alternating current. No one had yet invented
a motor that ran on AC, and Tesla was determined to do it.
It wasn't easy, though, and he struggled with the problem
for years. Meanwhile, in 1882, he got a job in Paris with
the Continental Edison Company, owned by the American
electrical pioneer Thomas Edison.

Tesla was 26 years old by then, tall and elegant. He
spoke at least half a dozen languages and could (and

did) quote great swaths of poetry from memory. He was also odd. He silently counted each step on his way to work in the morning. He disliked shaking hands, hated women's earrings, and couldn't bear to touch another person's hair. He had to calculate the volume of anything he ate or drank before he touched it. The obsessions stayed with him all his life, feeding the image of the mad inventor.

The oddness didn't affect his work or his inventions. In Paris, he finally solved the puzzle of a motor that would run on alternating current, and he began dreaming up related inventions. He did so well in his job that his boss urged him to go to the United States and meet Thomas Edison himself. Tesla took up the offer and arrived in New York in 1884 with a few cents in his pocket and a letter of introduction.

Father... the conditions for my survival are as follows:
1) i shall become an electrical engineer, not a priest
2) i will need breakfast in bed 3 days a week
3) i shall never ever clean up my room.

TESLA'S OBSESSIONS

He calculates the volume of everything he eats or drinks.

Just 50 mL of wine, 12 cm³ steak, and 8 cm³ mashed potatoes, please.

On his way to work every morning, he counts his steps in Serbian.

When he meets someone, he doesn't like to shake hands.

The Storekeeper Makes Light

Francis Hauksbee was a storekeeper with a passion for science. While he was assisting Isaac Newton in his studies of glass and air pumps in the early 1700s, he made a startling and accidental discovery. He had pumped the air out of a glass globe and was rotating it when he noticed a strange purple glow under his hands. Hauksbee realized he was seeing an effect of static electricity. He continued experimenting with static electricity and light for the next decade. His was the first serious study of what we now call neon lights.

NO MEETING OF MINDS

Tesla was thrilled to meet Edison. He hoped to share his excitement about his engine design, but Edison told him bluntly that working on alternating current was a waste of time. Still, he gave Tesla a job. Tesla quit a year later, after a fight about money, and set out to pursue his dream of powering the world with alternating current.

There was a lot at stake for both men. Edison had been working on a direct current system to replace gas lighting and candles with electrical lighting. He had already set up a couple of small, local systems, and he and his investors had plowed a lot of money into the project. They needed to expand if they were going to make money back.

Tesla was sure that alternating current was the way to go. He had his motor design, a string of new inventions, and a growing reputation in America, all of which led a group of investors to convince him it was time to set up his own company, the Tesla Electric Light Company. But his lack of business sense showed. In early 1886, they forced him out, and Tesla ended up working as a ditchdigger.

The Glowing Barometer

Jean Picard was a French astronomer who worked on the first science-based map of France. In 1675, he was carrying a barometer from one location to another in the dark of night. The barometer, designed to measure atmospheric pressure, was really just a glass tube partly filled with mercury.

When Picard accidentally joggled the mercury in the barometer, a glow appeared where the mercury met the empty space above it. Quite startled, he reported the phenomenon to his colleagues. Apart from playing with their barometers a bit to see if it would happen again (it did!), they appear to have done little more than make a brief note about the incident. It might be the first recorded scientific observation of electric light. The light was created when the mercury and glass were pulled apart by the joggling, releasing some electrons. The electrons collided with gas molecules, making them glow. It's basically the same process that makes neon lights glow.

Mon dieu!

barometer

THE BATTLE BEGINS

Tesla's ditchdigging career ended when another investor set him up in a laboratory. Finally, in 1888, Tesla built the motor he had dreamed of for so long, and it brought him an even bigger investor: George Westinghouse. Westinghouse, another electrical pioneer, had an AC-generating plant in Buffalo, New York, and he and Tesla made big plans to expand it and sell the electricity it produced.

Word of those plans reached Edison. Now, Edison was a tough competitor. He meant to make sure his company was the way of the future, and that way would be direct current. So he launched a nasty campaign to convince people that alternating current wasn't safe. An Edison company man went from town to town, giving talks and putting on public displays where he demonstrated the dangers of alternating current by electrocuting a variety of animals, including dogs, a horse, and even a circus elephant.

And now I will demonstrate the dangers of alternating current.

← metal sheet

The battle went on for years, with each side claiming its system was safer and better. Westinghouse almost lost his company, and Edison did lose his. It was taken over and renamed General Electric, a company that still exists today. Westinghouse's victory was complete in 1893, when his company won a contract to provide electricity for the Chicago World's Fair.

The Fair was an alternating-current extravaganza, with 180,000 glittering light bulbs, a giant Ferris wheel, moving sidewalks, and electric water fountains. Tesla himself put on stage shows with dazzling displays of electrical tricks and gizmos, indoor lightning, and cascades of sparks— demonstrating, spectacularly, that alternating current could be safe.

WINNER LOSES ALL

Tesla was a star, and loved it, but it didn't last. For a few years, he and Westinghouse prospered, building power stations and distribution systems until their generating plant at Niagara Falls provided one-fifth of all the electricity in the United States. Tesla had money, admiration, and honors.

He also had ideas. He filed the first radio patent, years before Marconi, who usually gets credit for inventing radio. He designed electrical components that are still used today, even in devices such as television sets that didn't exist in his time.

Tesla designed and built a radio-controlled boat, and then demonstrated it to a puzzled New York crowd in 1898. It was powered by a small battery (direct current, which should have pleased Edison) and controlled by a wireless radio transmitter that Tesla invented and operated. The boat was the beginning of modern robotics, although no one—except possibly Tesla—knew it at the time.

With the remote-controlled boat, Tesla was already ahead of his audience. He tried to sell it and other remote-controlled devices to the military, but they couldn't see the point. Today, of course, we send remote-controlled vehicles to the bottom of the ocean and into space. We have robots to do boring jobs, such as putting caps on bottles, and dangerous jobs, such as defusing bombs. We even play with robotic toys. At the beginning of the 20th century, however, that was beyond most people's imagining.

Not much was beyond Tesla's imagining. He built, designed, or talked about everything from a spark plug to global wireless communications systems. He tinkered with wireless power distribution, gave lectures on his idea for a worldwide information system that sounds remarkably like the internet, and laid out ideas for X-rays, radar, and electric vehicles. None of these ideas earned him money or brought him investors. He had moved too far, too fast.

When Nikola Tesla died, in 1943 in New York, he was thousands of dollars in debt. His closest companions were the hundreds of pigeons that he fed daily in the park, and the sick and injured pigeons he coaxed into his hotel room.

He understood us...

And we understood him

What will we do now?

TESLA'S BED

His ideas were brilliant

He was lonely, but he wasn't forgotten. A few friends from his Westinghouse days had chipped in to pay his monthly hotel bill. And, after he died, he was honored with a state funeral. More than 2,000 people attended, and the mayor of New York read a eulogy.

THE DISAPPEARING PAPERS

After Tesla's death, all his papers and belongings were seized by American government officials, and an electrical engineer working for the government was brought in to study them, possibly because Tesla had talked about weapons systems in his last years. The engineer concluded that there were no workable plans for weapons in the papers, but the government hung on to most of them for years. Some have never been released or have simply been lost in government storage, but people still comb through the papers that are available, looking for brilliant ideas that might yet come true.

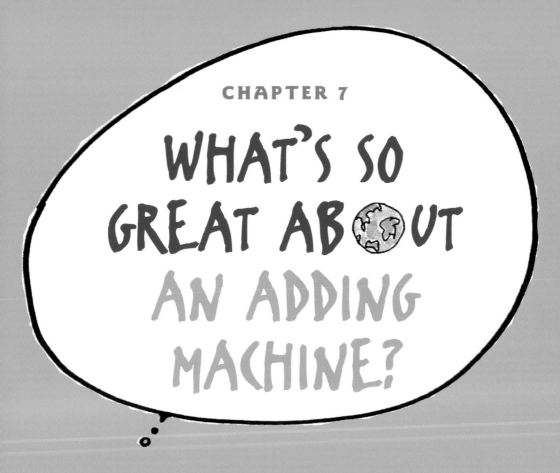

CHAPTER 7

WHAT'S SO GREAT ABOUT AN ADDING MACHINE?

Everyone knows what a computer is, right? It's an electronic brain, in a way. It can do all kinds of calculating, thinking, planning, and playing for us.

In 1820, the word meant something else entirely. A *computer* was a person who picked up extra money by doing basic mathematical calculations over and over and over again. The calculations were compiled in huge tables of numbers that were shortcuts for more complex calculations. They were used by engineers to calculate structural loads for bridges, by ocean navigators to figure out a ship's location, and by bankers, insurance agents, tax collectors, surveyors, and astronomers.

Important as they were, the tables were usually full of errors. The human computers made mistakes, because they were tired or bored or simply careless. More mistakes crept in when the tables were compiled and printed. The mistakes might be minor, or they might send a ship off course and onto a rock.

A Computer ~ 1822

ink →

= 1 × 1
1 + 984 1 =
= 16 + 3 + 2

many years ago we used our brains to add.

BUILDING AN INHUMAN COMPUTER

Careful users, like the astronomer John Herschel, checked the tables for accuracy. In the fall of 1821, he and his mathematician friend Charles Babbage were sitting in Babbage's house in London, painstakingly checking two sets of numbers from two different computers. The numbers should have matched, but they didn't. Exasperated, one of the men (neither could remember which) exclaimed that he wished someone would invent an engine to do the calculations.

A few weeks later, in December 1821, Babbage did invent it. Or, at least, he started to invent it. He called his idea the Difference Engine, and he worked on it and its successors, off and on, for the next 50 years. His designs pioneered many of the fundamental ideas behind modern computers.

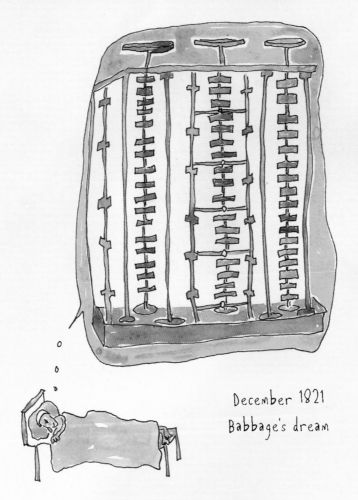

December 1821
Babbage's dream

Charles Babbage was 30 years old when he came up with the idea for the Difference Engine. Among his circle of friends were many of the leading young English scientists of the day, and he knew what they needed. A machine that did simple arithmetic—addition, subtraction, multiplication, and division—was not enough. They needed a machine that could do advanced calculations and get them right every time.

Babbage also realized that the machine had to do more than calculate. It had to print out its results, preferably in a form that would go straight to press. That would get rid of all the stages where the human-computer system introduced mistakes.

WHEELS UPON WHEELS

He thought and calculated and sketched ideas until he came up with a plan. His machine would be fully automatic. Once the operator set up the basic information, all he had to do was turn a crank to produce a series of calculated numbers—guaranteed correct. Babbage designed a machine to print the numbers on a roll of paper and press them into a soft mold to create the lead type for printing.

Electronics didn't exist yet, so the Difference Engine was entirely mechanical. That made it a huge challenge. It relied on thousands of small, toothed wheels engraved with the numbers zero to nine that interacted with each other to do the calculations. The idea was a bit like a bicycle lock, where you line up the numbers of the combination in order to take it apart—but on a much grander scale. Very grand, in fact. Babbage's engine needed more than 25,000 carefully engineered metal parts, and would end up as big as two double beds, legs and all.

The Scheutz Difference Engine

A Difference Engine was built in the 1800s, but not by Babbage. In 1834, a Swedish printer named Georg Scheutz read an article describing Babbage's machine and decided to try building his own. His son, Edvard, got involved and they plugged away at the idea for several years. By 1843, they had a working model with a printing mechanism. In 1850, the Swedish government gave them enough money to build a full-size machine. It was completed in 1853 and won a medal at the Paris Exhibition the next year. Babbage, who could be touchy, praised their work generously. The Scheutz Difference Engine had some success, but a glitch of some sort caused it to make occasional, unpredictable errors, and it eventually fell into disuse.

WORK GRINDS ON, AND ON

The next step was to build the Difference Engine. For that, Babbage needed two things: money and a first-rate machinist. He started with the money.

Babbage came from a wealthy family, but he had quarreled with his father and couldn't go to him for money. Babbage and his wife, between them, had enough to live comfortably and support their children, but there wasn't enough left over to build the Difference Engine. So, in 1823, Babbage appealed to the British prime minister for funds. Prime Minister Peel didn't see the point of the machine, but he was persuaded to hand over 1,500 pounds. It was enough to make a good start.

LONG TEMPER (good)→

MEDIUM TEMPER

SHORT TEMPER

JOSEPH CLEMENT'S TEMPER →

SPOT IN YOUR BRAIN THAT STORES YOUR TEMPER

← JOSEPH CLEMENT IS HIRED

Babbage used the money to hire the expert, and expensive, machinist Joseph Clement. Clement had a reputation for a short temper and brilliant workmanship. Babbage was no easier to get along with, especially after his wife died in 1827. He was proud, irritable, and he held a grudge. Although Clement and Babbage worked well together at first, they soon started arguing, mostly over money. The Difference Engine got more and more expensive, especially since Babbage kept tinkering with the design and adding to it, and Clement understandably refused to work without pay.

Babbage went back to the government for money several times, eventually prying a total of 9,000 pounds from two different prime ministers. That doesn't sound like much, but the modern equivalent in U.S. dollars would be well over $1 million. Still, it wasn't enough. Clement suspended work for a year when the money ran dry again. Then he and Babbage quarreled bitterly, and he quit altogether. Work on the Difference Engine stopped in 1833 and never restarted. The British government ended up paying for some of Babbage's debts and, in the end, put a total of 17,478 pounds into the project, enough to buy two warships—and all for nothing.

BABBAGE MOVES ON

By then, Babbage was sick of the Difference Engine. He was already thinking about a new and more ambitious machine: the Analytical Engine. It would be able to do far more complicated calculations than the Difference Engine, and even perform calculations based on its earlier calculations.

To tell the engine what to do and in what order, Babbage borrowed a system from England's textile mills: punch cards. Instructions would be fed into the engine on a wide ribbon of cards with punched holes that configured the machine's metal parts. It was, basically, a mechanical version of an early computer—right down to the punch cards, which were used to deliver instructions to the first modern computers.

Babbage hired a new machinist (and didn't fight with him), and together they produced what Babbage called his Scribbling Books. They were actually 7,000 large sheets of notes and sketches outlining several versions of the Analytical Engine. In addition, the two men created about 500 design drawings, each the size of a desk, and another 1,000 sheets of notes about the drawings. All of that paper ended up in the possession of the Science Museum in London, and researchers there have been poring over the notes for years, trying to understand Babbage's dream.

For it remained a dream. The Analytical Engine was never built. The British government was not prepared to spend any more money on Babbage's ideas. Nevertheless, Babbage didn't give up on the idea. Almost until he died in 1871, just short of his 80th birthday, Babbage was still tinkering with the design of his Analytical Engine.

Babbage's Sidekick

Charles Babbage designed the Analytical Engine, but Ada Lovelace was the visionary who understood what it might do. Ada, Countess of Lovelace, was the daughter of the famous English poet Lord Byron. She was an impressive mathematician who worked with Babbage on his punch-card instruction system. He designed the machine to work with numbers, but Ada realized that numbers are just symbols, like letters or musical notes. The Analytical Engine could be programmed to process any kind of symbol, even to make music, she wrote.

Ada Lovelace died young, while Babbage was still trying unsuccessfully to find money to build his Analytical Engine, and she never got the chance to test her idea. However, her notes about the Analytical Engine's capacity were the first public explanation of computer programming, and a programming language developed in the late 1970s was named Ada in her honor.

THE ENGINES RISE AGAIN

Babbage's work was largely forgotten until after the computer was reinvented, this time based on electricity, in the 1930s. Since then, however, his work and his papers have been rediscovered.

In 1991, researchers at the Science Museum built a perfectly functioning Difference Engine. It is based on Babbage's revised design, which involved only about 7,000 parts, and it works beautifully. Nine years later, the Science Museum completed the Difference Engine's printer. And in 2010, Babbage enthusiasts associated with the museum launched a 10-year project to build the Babbage Analytical Engine—at last.

From Pocket Pistol to Pocket Calculator

In the 1600s, during the short period when England had no monarch, Samuel Morland had a brief career as a spy and a double agent, spying for both the royalist party and Oliver Cromwell's non-royalist government. Near the end of his time as a double agent, he was almost caught. Called to a secret meeting with his boss on the government side and, as he wrote later, fully expecting to have to fight for his life, Morland tucked a pistol in each pocket. Fortunately, he didn't have to fire them. A little fast talking and some dramatic pistol-waving got him out of trouble.

Less than a year later, in 1660, the monarchy was restored and Morland got out of the spy business. He began inventing and building mechanical calculators, three altogether: an adding machine, a multiplying machine, and a device that did trigonometry. The adding machine, about the size of a cell phone, may have been the first true pocket calculator. It was pretty, but it wasn't very useful since it did only parts of the calculations. Morland also wrote a book about mechanical calculators, the only one in English until Babbage wrote about his own engines 200 years later.

CHAPTER 8

THE BIRDS FALL SILENT

In the late 1950s, an airplane swooped low over wetlands near the American city of Boston and spewed out a cloud of the insecticide DDT. It was part of a government program to control the mosquitoes that thrived there.

Within days, people who lived near the wetlands found dying birds in their yards and around their bird baths and bird feeders. Grasshoppers, bees, and many other harmless insects had disappeared. The mosquitoes, however, were alive and well and just as hungry as ever, apparently unbothered by the chemical designed to kill them.

A woman who lived near the wetlands wrote a letter to her friend, the famous science writer Rachel Carson, asking for suggestions about who to contact to get the spraying stopped. Carson, who was already researching the effects of insecticides, went one step further. She wrote a book.

The book got her in trouble—lots of trouble—but it helped change the way we think about both chemicals and the environment.

WORDS AND BIRDS

It wasn't Rachel Carson's first book. She had been writing for most of her life. Born in 1907, Carson grew up just outside a small town near the manufacturing city of Pittsburgh, Pennsylvania. Her brother and sister were much older and her father was away a lot, so she spent a lot of time with her mother. Carson's mother, Maria, was a passionate naturalist and taught her daughter to identify plants, birds, and animals. She also encouraged her to read and write. That suited Rachel just fine. She spent hours and days exploring the woods and fields around her home, often with just her dog for company, and she wrote about what she saw.

When she was nine, she gave her father a handmade book with a drawing of an animal and a short poem on each page. When she was eleven, she began sending her stories to magazines, and several were published. When she was fourteen, a magazine paid her three dollars for a story. Carson was officially a professional writer.

NEW FASCINATIONS

Rachel Carson always knew she was going to be a writer, but in university she discovered that she wanted to be a scientist too. In the end, she became both.

She took a biology course—simply because she had to—and discovered a passion for science. Carson decided to become a marine biologist and study life in the ocean. It was a bold ambition for a young woman in the 1920s. Not many women studied science in those days, and even fewer found jobs as scientists. Besides, Carson had never even seen the sea. She fell in love with it entirely through books and poems.

Still, she earned an advanced degree in zoology and aquatic biology, and she conducted research at Woods Hole, a famous marine biology research center in Massachusetts. There she roamed the seaside, peered into tide pools, poked along rocky shores, and watched the tides roll in and out. The sea was just as wonderful as she had imagined, and the animals that made the sea their home were beyond her imaginings.

Not long after Carson graduated came the 1929 stock market crash and the beginnings of the Great Depression. Carson's family, never wealthy, was suddenly very poor. The whole family—mother, father, brother, sister, and two nieces—moved in with her. Suddenly, she was the family breadwinner. She needed a job, soon!

BREAKING DOWN BARRIERS

And she found one. Rachel Carson was the first woman biologist ever hired by the American Department of Fisheries. However, she might never have got the job if she hadn't been a writer. Her new boss was supposed to produce a radio series and some brochures to explain fisheries science to the public. He had no idea what to do, but Carson did. In fact, a brochure she produced was so good that her boss encouraged her to submit it to a major magazine—and it sold.

Carson worked for government for almost 20 years. She needed the money. Her father had died and her brother moved away, but for the rest of her life she supported other family members, including her adopted son, Roger.

Carson also continued to write magazine articles, mainly about the natural world and the sea. Gradually, she earned a reputation for making science understandable, exciting, and even beautiful to a non-scientific audience. She began to write books—and there she struck gold. Her second book, *The Sea Around Us*, published in 1951, was a huge success. It made so much money that Carson quit her government job to write full time.

THE SILENT KILLER

Carson wrote other books about her great passion, the sea, but the book that she's remembered for—the book that changed so much—was the one she didn't want to write at all. *Silent Spring* described how manufactured pesticides, particularly DDT, were working their way through every kind of life, from mosquitoes to humans.

All through the 1930s and 1940s, scientists had been inventing new chemicals to do everything from cure diseases to clean your oven. By the 1950s, people were enchanted by chemicals.

The huge companies that made them promised a rosy future without insect damage, insect-spread diseases, or even annoying bug bites. Agriculture and health specialists, crop and insect scientists, farmers, and gardeners were just as enthusiastic. One advertisement even showed a housewife spraying the inside of her kitchen cupboards with DDT.

What is DDT?

DDT is short for the mouth-filling word dichloro-diphenyl-trichloroethane, a chemical created in a lab in 1874. In the 1940s, it was used to kill insects, especially the lice, fleas, and mosquitoes that spread disease among soldiers fighting in the Second World War. After the war, DDT was used in many countries to attack insects that threatened health, crops, gardens, or human comfort.

A future free of irritating bugs sounded fine to most people. Today, we understand that nature is a network of ecosystems, where all forms of life—including humans—are interconnected. But that's a fairly new way to see the world. In the 1950s, most people thought of nature as separate from humans. Removing a whole group of animals didn't seem like a bad idea, especially if they were mosquitoes.

Biologists, however, had been thinking about the natural world in a new way. Around the 1930s, a few biologists, including some of Rachel Carson's colleagues, began looking at ecosystems: food webs, habitats, and all the relationships that link plants and animals, including insects, together. As insect-killing chemicals spread in the 1940s and 1950s, the biologists wondered what happened to ecosystems after the insects died.

POISON IN THE SYSTEM

What the biologists discovered alarmed them. The
chemicals didn't vanish with the insects. Instead, they were
passed from one animal to the next, through food webs.
DDT in an insect's body was transferred to the fish or songbird that ate it, then to the seal that ate the fish or the falcon
that ate the songbird, and eventually to whatever ate the
seal or falcon. Humans were part of the food chain too, and
scientists found DDT and other chemicals in people's bodies,
even in mothers' milk. (Today, these chemicals are called
persistent organic pollutants—POPs, for short—and they're
recognized as an international problem.)

The more the researchers learned, the more they worried.
Rachel Carson was one of the worriers. By the time her friend
wrote about the dying birds near Boston, Carson had been
collecting research about chemicals in the environment for

years. She felt strongly that someone should write a book
explaining the problem to the public, but she didn't want
to be the writer. It would mean months or years of work.

And it would mean a battle. The chemical industry had
supporters in government, agriculture, and research. Carson
was a quiet, private person. A public battle with big business,
politicians, and other scientists was the last thing she wanted.

But try as she might to convince other well-known writers
to tackle the book, no one did. Finally, Rachel Carson
decided it was up to her.

Rachel, dear, you know how
busy I am . . . I have rugby
tonight, checkers tomorrow. . .

Here's all my research,
Jeremy. You HAVE to
write this book!

TAKING ON THE BIG BOYS

Carson spent years reading scientific papers, exchanging letters with the top scientists in the field, and writing. It was hard work, made even harder by her health. She had cancer, and it was getting worse, but she was determined to finish the book. She told only a few friends about her illness and swore them to secrecy.

Silent Spring was published in September 1962. Its title came from the opening chapter, where Carson described an imaginary town, sometime in the near future, where a cloud of DDT has killed everything, including the birds, crickets, and frogs that make the music of spring. The book explained how DDT worked, how it moved through the environment, and some of the damage it caused. Carson argued that these impacts should be researched, understood, and considered when making a decision to use DDT and similar chemicals. *Silent Spring* was well written, thoroughly researched, and— for many readers—convincing.

Just as Carson had expected, the chemical manufacturers and their supporters were furious. After all, their wonderful new chemicals were going to make a better world. Surely, they couldn't be causing actual harm.

The trouble was, Carson had done her research well. It was hard to argue with her book, so the industry and its supporters attacked her instead.

The attacks were vicious and personal. She was no scientist, some said, and couldn't understand the issues. Her book should be classified as science fiction, not science. She belonged to

a "cult" of organic gardeners and bird lovers who wanted to destroy modern agriculture, some critics said. She was even called a Communist (an illegal political party in the United States), and an American law agency investigated her as a threat to the food supply.

Some people attacked Carson simply because she was a woman, calling her hysterical and irrational and dismissing her book as an emotional rant. At a time when society expected most women to marry and have children, one man— a former senior official in the United States government— wondered why an unmarried woman with no biological children was so concerned about human genetics.

Al-Jahiz and the Animals

About 1,200 years ago, the Arab writer and philosopher
known as Al-Jahiz was interested in many of the same ideas
Charles Darwin and Rachel Carson explored centuries later.
Al-Jahiz lived from 776 CE to about 869 CE in what is now
Iraq. He was born poor, probably the descendant of an African
slave, but he became a famous writer with about 200 books
to his credit. One of his most famous works was the *Book of
Animals,* a seven-volume collection of writings about animals,
from proverbs and poetry to his own observations. He wrote
about food chains, in which smaller animals are eaten by
ever-larger animals, all the way from minnows to sharks. He
also speculated about how the behavior and even appearance
of animals can be affected by their environment. In fact, the
Book of Animals contained ideas that wouldn't become major
concerns of European science for almost a thousand years.

WEATHERING THE STORM

Through all the criticism, Carson remained calm and
polite. She patiently explained, again and again in interviews
and speeches, that she hadn't suggested a complete ban on
DDT and other pesticides, just more care in their use and
more research into their effects.

People listened, and they bought the book. Forty thousand
copies of *Silent Spring* had already been ordered and paid for
before the book was even published. It was translated into
many other languages and became an international best seller.

Carson was asked to testify before an American government committee studying the environment, and the American president, John F. Kennedy, was among the people who praised the book.

One of its most enthusiastic attackers was Robert White-Stevens, a scientist who worked for a chemical company. In the fall of 1962, he made more than two dozen speeches attacking Carson and her book, calling her "a fanatic defender of the cult of the balance of nature." Several months after *Silent Spring* appeared, a respected news program on American television aired interviews with Carson, White-Stevens, and several other critics of the book.

The Lorax Wins the Day

Are you a Dr. Seuss fan? You might not realize that Dr. Seuss was a trailbreaker—and not just by creating weird creatures and strange rhymes. Like Rachel Carson, he wrote about ecosystems and what happens when you tamper with them—but his writing was aimed at young children.

In 1971, less than a decade after Carson's *Silent Spring*, Dr. Seuss published *The Lorax*. It's the story of a fuzzy little creature called a Lorax, a beautiful forest of Truffula trees, and the Once-ler, whose factory used up all the Truffulas, destroyed the forest, and drove away the creatures that depended on it. *The Lorax* is a miniature picture of how an ecosystem works, written at a time when it still wasn't common for schools to teach about food webs, ecosystems, and pollution. Dr. Seuss managed to explain them in terms that small children could understand—and they did. But their parents weren't always happy about that.

In 1989, the parents of a Grade Two student in Laytonville, California, campaigned to have *The Lorax* banned from local schools because it showed the timber industry in a bad light. It wasn't banned, but it was removed from school reading lists in the town. Timber industry supporters tried to get other communities do the same, but without much success. *The Lorax* survived and remained so popular that it has even been made into a movie. Twice.

The interview with Carson had been recorded at her home because she was too ill to travel. Nevertheless, viewers saw a quiet and dignified woman who clearly understood her subject. This was not the hysterical fanatic her critics described. White-Stevens warned, "If man were to faithfully follow the teachings of Miss Carson, we would return to the Dark Ages, and the insects and diseases and vermin would once again inherit the earth." However, he and his fellow critics failed to convince the program's host or its audience. The next day, a member of the American Senate said the program showed the "appalling lack of information about environmental hazards."

A STEP ON THE ROAD

Silent Spring made a difference. By the early 1970s, DDT was banned in the United States, Canada, and many other countries. It's still used in some parts of the world, often to fight the mosquitoes that spread malaria, but not as heavily as in the past. Since *Silent Spring*, governments have created departments of the environment and laws to oversee things that might cause environmental damage. In fact, *Silent Spring* marks the beginning of the modern environmental movement.

Rachel Carson lived long enough to see the beginning of that change, before she died of cancer in the spring of 1964. She didn't see the end, however, because the battle isn't over. Harmful chemicals are still in use, and many that were used in the past still show up in the environment. And scientists are still trying to understand their full impacts.

CAN YOU SPOT THE TRAILBREAKERS?

How do you spot the trailbreakers and the trailblockers?
It's easy to look back and say Copernicus was a trailbreaker.
It's even easy to see that the doctors offended by Semmelweis's
handwashing rules were trailblockers. It's not so easy to identify
the sides, however, when you're in the middle of the battle.

The battle itself might be very easy to spot. One of the
biggest battles today is over climate change. Climate scientists
are the trailbreakers. Almost all of them agree that the world is
warming, that the change is dangerous, and that human actions
are responsible. But that's an uncomfortable idea. If we accept
it, that means we have to do something about it. We have to
change the way we think about the world and the way we act,
the way we travel and heat or cool our houses, even the foods
we eat and the products we buy.

So there are trailblockers in the climate change battle too—both organizations and individuals. Some depend on the fuels that are causing climate change. Some are afraid of losing the things that make life comfortable. Some don't believe that humans could have such power. Some just don't want to think about anything so unpleasant. And some have been convinced by other trailblockers—almost always people who aren't climate scientists—that climate change is a hoax or an evil conspiracy.

The struggle between climate change trailbreakers and trailblockers is taking place in plain sight, all around us. You can see it on news broadcasts, in magazines and newspapers, in books, and on the internet. You can even be part of it.

But how do you know which side is right? The best approach is to follow Rachel Carson's example. Keep asking questions, and look for information from the right people. If the issue is climate change, look for a climate scientist. If the issue is endangered frogs, then a frog biologist is your best bet. If the issue is . . .

Well, what is the next issue? Look around you. Listen, watch, read, and think. Can you spot the next big idea that the world is not quite ready to accept? A new kind of energy? A solution to climate change? A way to feed the world? Or something else. Something entirely unexpected.

Maybe you'll be the one to come up with the next good, true, world-shaking idea. Maybe you'll be the trailbreaker. It won't be easy, breaking trail, but it will be important. Good luck!

APPENDIX: THE PEOPLE

Chapter 1
Nicolaus Copernicus
  (1473–1543), *Polish*
Claudius Ptolemy
  (ca 90 CE–ca 168 CE), *Greek-Egyptian*
Georg Joachim Rheticus
  (1514–1574), *German*
Galileo Galilei
  (1564–1642), *Italian*
Aristarchus of Samos
  (310 BCE–ca 230 BCE), *Greek*
Aryabhata
  (476–550), *Indian*
Caroline Herschel
  (1750–1848), *German*

Chapter 2
Alfred Wegener
  (1880–1930), *German*
James Hutton
  (1726–1797), *Scottish*
Charles Lyell
  (1797–1875), *British*
Abraham Ortelius
  (1527–1598), *Flemish*
Antonio Snider-Pellegrini
  (1802–1885), *French*
Marie Tharp
  (1920–2006), *American*

Chapter 3
Ignaz Philipp Semmelweis
  (1818–1865), *Hungarian*
Louis Pasteur
  (1822–1895), *French*
Joseph Lister
  (1827–1912), *English*
Robert Koch
  (1843–1910), *German*
Alexander Gordon
  (1752–1799), *Scottish*
Filippo Pacini
  (1812–1883), *Italian*

Chapter 4
Charles Darwin
  (1809–1882), *English*
Jean-Baptiste Lamarck
  (1744–1829), *French*
Alfred Russel Wallace
  (1823–1913), *British*
Robert Chambers
  (1802–1871), *Scottish*
Mary Anning
  (1799–1847), *English*

FURTHER READING

Christie, Peter. *50 Climate Questions: A Blizzard of Blistering Facts*. Toronto: Annick Press, 2012.

Jennings, Gael. *Bloody Moments: Highlights from the Astonishing History of Medicine*. Toronto: Annick Press, 2000.

Johnstone, Michael. *History News: Space News*. Somerville, Massachusetts: Candlewick Press, 2001.

Locker, Thomas. *Rachel Carson: Preserving a Sense of Wonder*. Golden, Colorado: Fulcrum Books, 2009.

Loxton, Daniel. *Evolution: How We and All Living Things Came to Be*. Toronto: Kids Can Press, 2010.

McPherson, Stephanie Sammartino. *War of the Currents: Thomas Edison vs Nikola Tesla*. Minneapolis, Minnesota: Lerner Publishing Group, 2012.

Raum, Elizabeth. *The History of the Computer*. Portsmouth, New Hampshire: Heinemann Library, 2007.

Rinard, Judith. *Book of Flight: The Smithsonian National Air and Space Museum*. Richmond Hill, Ontario: Firefly Books, 2007.

Swanson, Diane. *Nibbling on Einstein's Brain: The Good, the Bad, and the Bogus in Science*. Revised edition. Toronto: Annick Press, 2009.

Thornhill, Jan. *This is My Planet: The Kids' Guide to Global Warming*. Toronto: Maple Tree Press, 2007.

Young, Greg. *Alfred Wegener: Pioneer of Plate Tectonics*. North Mankato, Minnesota: Capstone Publishers, 2009.

SELECTED BIBLIOGRAPHY

"Alexander Gordon of Aberdeen." *Canadian Medical Association Journal* 19, no. 2
(Aug. 1928): 218.

"Alfred Lothar Wegener: Moving continents." United States Geological Survey website.
Retrieved May 7, 2012, from http://pubs.usgs.gov/gip/dynamic/wegener.html

"Alfred Wegener (1880-1930)." University of California Museum of Paleontology
website. Retrieved May 8, 2012, from http://www.ucmp.berkeley.edu/history/
wegener.html

"First manned flight recreated." BBC News website, July 5, 2003. Retrieved May 12,
2012, from http://news.bbc.co.uk/go/pr/fr/-/2/hi/uk_news/3047164.stm

"Ignaz Semmelweis (1818-65)." Wellcome Library, London (website). Retrieved May 9,
2012, from http://www.sciencemuseum.org.uk/broughttolife.aspx

"Marie Tharp Bio." Mary Sears Woman Pioneer in Oceanography Award (website).
Retrieved July 24, 2012, from http://www.whoi.edu/sbl/liteSite.do?litesiteid=9092&
articleId=13407

"Remembered: Marie Tharp, pioneering mapmaker of the ocean floor." Columbia News
(website), Aug. 24, 2006/last modified Nov. 14, 2007. Retrieved July 24, 2012,
from http://www.columbia.edu/cu/news/06/08/tharp.html

"Tesla: master of lightning." PBS website, 2004. Retrieved May 13, 2012, from http://
www.pbs.org/tesla

"The birth of electrostatics." *Physics Today*, Sept. 2006.

Ackroyd, J. A. D. "Sir George Cayley, the Father of Aeronautics. Part 1. The invention
of the aeroplane." *Notes and Records of the Royal Society of London* 56, no. 2
(May 2002): 167–181.

Ackroyd, J. A. D. "Sir George Cayley, the Father of Aeronautics. Part 2. Cayley's
aeroplanes." *Notes and Records of the Royal Society of London*, Vol. 56, No. 3
(Sept. 2002), pp. 333–348.

Bailey, Ronald H. "The wizard who electrified the world." *American History*, June 2010,
53–59.

Balchin, Jon. *Quantum Leaps: 100 Scientists Who Changed the World*. London:
Arcturus Publishing Limited, 2004.

Burke, James. *The Day the Universe Changed*. Boston, Toronto: Little, Brown and
Company, 1985.

Carson, Rachel. *Silent Spring*. Boston, New York: Houghton Mifflin Company, 2002.
Originally published 1962.

Conniff, Richard. "When continental drift was considered pseudoscience." *Smithsonian
Magazine*, June 2012.

Cork, David P., Pinckney J. Maxwell IV, and Charles J. Yeo. "Remembering Semmelweis:
Hand hygiene and its importance in today's clinical practice." *American Surgeon*,
Jan. 2011, 123.

Darwin, Charles. *The Origin of Species*. [Republication of 1859 first edition with additions from sixth edition.] New York: Gramercy Books, 1979.

Dodge, N.S. "Charles Babbage." *IEEE Annals of the History of Computing*, Oct.–Dec. 2000, 22–43.

Fara, Patricia. *Pandora's Breeches: Women, Science and Power in the Enlightenment*. London: Pimlico, 2004.

Fara, Patricia. *Science: A Four Thousand Year History*. Oxford: Oxford University Press, 2009.

Freeman, Martha, ed. *Always, Rachel: The Letters of Rachel Carson and Dorothy Freeman, 1952–1964, The Story of a Remarkable Friendship*. Boston: Beacon Press, 1995.

Fuegi, John, and Jo Francis. "Lovelace & Babbage and the creation of the 1843 'Notes.'" *IEEE Annals of the History of Computing* 25, no. 4 (Oct. 2003): 16–26.

Gibbs-Smith, Charles H. "Sir George Cayley: 'Father of Aerial Navigation' (1773-1857)." *Notes and Records of the Royal Society of London* 17, no. 1 (May 1962): 36–56.

Graham, Frank, Jr. "Fifty years after *Silent Spring*, assault on science continues." Yale Environment 360, June 21, 2012. Retrieved July 20, 2012, from http://e360.yale.edu/feature/fifty_years_after_rachel_carsons_silent_spring_assacult_on_science_continues/2544/

Graham, Frank, Jr. *Since Silent Spring*. Boston: Houghton Mifflin Company, 1970.

Hathaway, Nancy. *The Friendly Guide to the Universe*. New York: Penguin Books, 1994.

Hayashi, Takao. "Aryabhata I." *Britannica Biographies*, Jan. 12, 2011.

Heath, Thomas. *The Copernicus of Antiquity (Aristarchus of Samos)*. London, Society for Promoting Christian Knowledge; New York, The Macmillan Company, 1920.

Highfield, Roger. "Zeros to heroes: the man who learned to fly." *New Scientist*, Sept. 16, 2010.

Hinkle, Annette. "50 Years of 'Silent Spring.'" *The Sag Harbor Express*, April 25, 2012. Retrieved May 23, 2012, from http://sagharboronline.com/sagharborexpress/arts/50-years-of-silent-spring-17251

Hughes, Patrick. "The meteorologist who started a revolution." *Weatherwise*, April/May 1994.

Jones, Glyn. "Babbage: architect of modern computing." *New Scientist*, June 29, 1991.

Jonnes, Jill. *Empires of Light: Edison, Tesla, Westinghouse, and the Race to Electrify the World*. New York: Random House, 2003.

Kuhn, Thomas S. *The Structure of Scientific Revolutions*. Third edition. Chicago: The University of Chicago Press, 1996.

Lane, Christopher. "Evolution before Darwin." *Huffington Post*, Mar. 27, 2012. Retrieved from http://www.huffingtonpost.com/christopher-lane/evolution-before-darwin_b_1371246.html

Lienhard, John H. "The flying monk." *Engines of Our Ingenuity* (website). Retrieved Dec. 7, 2011, from http://www.uh.edu/engines/epi3.htm

Loudon, Irvine. "Semmelweis and his thesis." *Journal of The Royal Society of Medicine* 98, no. 12 (Dec. 2005): 555.

Lytle, Mark Hamilton. *The Gentle Subversive: Rachel Carson, Silent Spring, and the Rise of the Environmental Movement.* New York, Oxford: Oxford University Press, 2007.

Mann, Michael E. *The Hockey Stick and the Climate Wars.* New York: Columbia University Press, 2012.

McGowan, Christopher. *The Dragon Seekers.* Cambridge, MA: Perseus Publishing, 2001.

McKie, Robin. "Rachel Carson and the legacy of *Silent Spring.*" *The Observer,* May 27, 2012.

Monahan, John. *They Called Me Mad.* New York: Berkley Books, 2010.

Pannekoek, A. *A History of Astronomy.* New York: Dover Publications, Inc., 1961.

Paschke, Jean. "Sir George Cayley, the father of aviation." *British Heritage,* Sept. 2007, 43.

Quammen, David. "Mr. Darwin's abominable volume: an essay." *The Virginia Quarterly Review,* 2006, 4–31.

Rajaraman, V. "Charles Babbage—a misunderstood genius." *Resonance: Journal of Science Education,* June 2002, 2–3.

Rajvanshi, Anil K. "Nikola Tesla—the creator of the electric age." *Resonance: Journal of Science Education,* March 2007, 4–12.

Repcheck, Jack. *The Man Who Found Time: James Hutton and the Discovery of the Earth's Antiquity.* Cambridge, MA: Perseus Publishing, 2003.

Snyder, Laura J. *The Philosophical Breakfast Club.* New York: Broadway Paperbacks, 2011.

Swade, Doron D. "The construction of Charles Babbage's Difference Engine No. 2." *IEEE Annals of the History of Computing,* July–Sept. 2005, 70–88.

Swade, Doron. "Building Babbage's dream machine." *New Scientist,* June 29, 1991.

Switek, Brian. *Written in Stone: Evolution, the Fossil Record, and Our Place in Nature.* New York: Bellevue Literary Press, 2010.

van Andel, P. "Semmelweis and puerperal fever." *Journal of Psychosomatic Obstetrics and Gynecology* 22 (Mar. 2001): 3–5.

Weeks, Linton. "The CBS Report that helped 'Silent Spring' be heard." *Washington Post,* Mar. 21, 2007.

White, Michael. *Acid Tongues and Tranquil Dreamers.* New York: William Morrow, 2001.

William of Malmesbury. *De Gestis Regum Anglorum,* Vol. I. Ed. William Stubbs (London, 1887), 276–277.

Zimmer, Carl. *Evolution: The Triumph of an Idea.* New York: Harper Perennial, 2006.

INDEX

ACKNOWLEDGMENTS

There's a saying that it takes a village to raise a child. Well, it takes at least part of a village to produce a book. Here are some of the people who helped produce this one.

Thanks to Patrick Daley, who helped with the research and did a wonderful job of digging up information about people most history books pass over.

Thanks to Andrew Ede, science historian at the University of Alberta, who reviewed the manuscript and provided both much-needed corrections and much-welcomed suggestions— including that I write a chapter about Rachel Carson. Thanks also to Joan Eamer, biologist and editor, for reviewing the Rachel Carson chapter.

Thanks to Concordia University College of Alberta for access to their research resources.

Thanks, of course, to the folk at Annick Press, especially Paula Ayer, who has been a pleasure to work with.

And finally, thanks to illustrator extraordinaire Sa Boothroyd, who makes everything more fun.

ABOUT THE AUTHOR

Claire Eamer is sure that she arrived (in Saskatoon, Canada) before the world was ready for her. She was clearly meant to be an exobiologist on a research base orbiting Europa, the ice-covered moon of Jupiter, studying the organisms living deep in Europa's oceans. Since that opportunity hasn't arisen (yet), she is a science writer, fascinated by all things scientific, but especially strange creatures. She particularly likes giant ground sloths and deep-ocean worms. And pretty much everything in between, actually.

Claire's previous books for Annick Press have received many awards and honors. They include *The World in Your Lunch Box*, also illustrated by Sa Boothroyd, and *Lizards in the Sky*. She lives in Whitehorse, Yukon, in northwest Canada.

ABOUT THE ILLUSTRATOR

Sa Boothroyd went to art school in London, England, sold etchings and woodblock prints in a small town in Quebec, Canada, and now lives in the village of Gibsons, in British Columbia, Canada, where she paints in her studio/gallery overlooking the harbor. Sa's unique style combines a wry sense of humor and drawing with her left (non-dominant) hand. In her spare time, Sa swims and bikes to retain her sanity. *Before the World Was Ready* is the second book she has illustrated for Annick Press.

If you liked "Before the World Was Ready," check out these books by the same author:

The World in Your Lunch Box: The Wacky History and Weird Science of Everyday Foods

BY CLAIRE EAMER   ART BY SA BOOTHROYD

paperback $14.95 | hardcover $22.95

*Eureka! Children's Book Award, Silver

"A smart and savory feast sure to prompt discussion and debate among readers."—*ForeWord Reviews*

"Elevat(es) the mundane into the realm of fascinating science and pop history."—*Booklist*

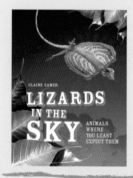

Lizards in the Sky: Animals Where You Least Expect Them

BY CLAIRE EAMER

paperback $12.95 | hardcover $21.95

"An enjoyable and fascinating title."—*School Library Journal*

"This well-researched book...will surprise and delight readers who are curious about the natural world."—*Resource Links*

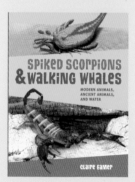

Spiked Scorpions and Walking Whales: Modern Animals, Ancient Animals, and Water

BY CLAIRE EAMER

paperback $9.95 | hardcover $19.95

"The vibrant presentation will draw in browsers who will find fascinating examples of evolution at work."—*Kirkus Reviews*

"Highly entertaining, engaging and educational...an absolute must-read."—*CM Magazine*